From
The Fallacy
of Economics
to
Climate Change

Chen Z X

CONTENTS

1

AN UNTOLD TRUTH

As a discipline that no one top university in the world fails to offer, economics has its origin in ancient Greece, where Xenophon (430–354 BC) wrote a treatise titled *Oeconomicus*. The study included the roles of men and women in domestic affairs, the control of slaves, and the use of farming technology.

After close to twenty-five hundred years of development, the key concern of the discipline is no longer about the management of individual households. A significant part of its field now covers how to manage and raise the economic welfare of an entire nation, i.e., *economic management*.

At its core, economists attempt to use theories to analyze the behaviors of people and then to predict their decisions and choices. One of the fundamental topics in their study is about *how price is determined*, where Alfred Marshall (1842–1942) is a key contributor.

As a professor teaching at Cambridge University from 1885 to 1908, Marshall managed to convince the institution to set up a new and independent program for economics, which, until 1903, had only been a branch of philosophy.

Though not many people are aware of Marshall's contribution in helping the discipline gain autonomy, they should probably find this familiar:

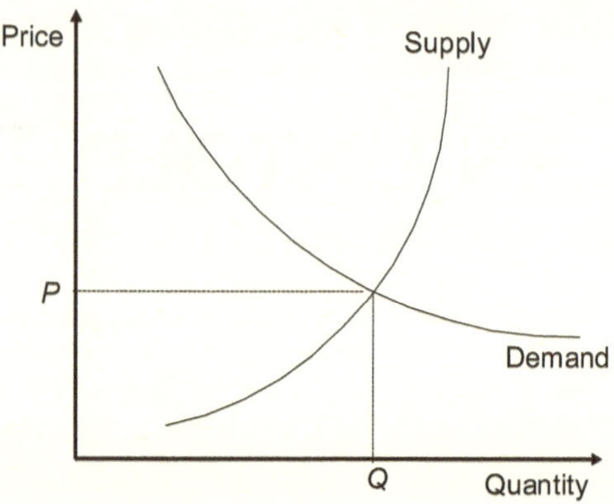

This is the iconic demand and supply curve that we can find across the entire discipline. They are based on the concept of *marginal analysis* developed by Marshall in his *Principles of Economics*, a book that was first published in 1890 and saw eight editions.

According to Marshall, people would have so-called utility or, in laymen's terms, pleasure to enjoy when consuming a good. Since his *law of diminishing returns* says marginal utility—or the additional pleasure to be enjoyed by us—will always become lower and lower when more and more units of a good are consumed, there is only one way for producers to get consumers to buy more and more units of their good. They have to let the price fall lower and lower. As such, the demand curve for a good will be plotted sloping downward from left to right.

As for the supply curve, Marshall used marginal cost to explain its shape. To supply more of a good, producers would need to secure more and more resources. When they produced more, the demand for the factors of production would bid up their prices. Given that they didn't set up the plants with the intention of suffering losses, producers would have to charge a price that was higher when more of the good was produced. That's why the supply curve is drawn sloping upward from left to right.

Basically, we can consider the diagram as a "market" for any good that we name, where all consumers are represented by one curve and all producers will be in the other. When these two curves are crossed, we'll be able to get something that sounds as though "it's best not to be disturbed," i.e., *the state of equilibrium*. From here on, we'll be able to foretell what will happen to the equilibrium quantity and equilibrium price of a good when its demand and/or supply changes. It can be done by "shifting" curve(s).

Before Marshall's introduction of using diagrams, the works of economists heretofore had been expressed solely in words. Whether it is explained by essays, plotting a few curves, or the combination of both, there is an obvious fact about "price" that this group of scholars has been completely oblivious of for centuries.

Long before the dawn of civilization, men had already known how to harvest more than what they needed for themselves—to generate surpluses—for them to *exchange* (or *trade*). Early on, most trade consisted of agricultural products, domestic surplus, catches of marine life, and handmade goods.

Today, the list is up to one's imagination, where human organs could be sold or a surrogate mother could be arranged.

In its earliest form, goods were exchanged for goods without using any form of medium. Such a system of trade is called *barter*.

It must have been extremely inconvenient for men living in ancient times. To get something in return, they had to wait for the right type of good to appear at the right place and at the right time, yet they still had to figure out how to "value" the objects of exchange.

To eliminate this kind of tricky issue once and for all, our ancestors in every part of the world, remarkably, all came up with the same ingenious idea. They used another *physical object*, or *medium*, when conducting exchanges.

The median of exchange is what all men around the world work so hard for every single day. A few are so desperate for money that they cheat, steal, extort, rob, kidnap, beg, and even resort to murder. Some therefore consider the median to be the root of all evil. But to Christopher Columbus (1451–1506), "discoverer" of America and brutal conqueror of native peoples, money "could get souls into paradise"[1]

In barter, price obviously *must be totally out of the picture*. Will this observation be any different with the presence of a medium of exchange?

When you enter into a Starbucks store, you'll surely find a board behind the counter listing the types and sizes of all beverages it is offering with their respective prices. If you order a cup of 12-ounce cappuccino at $2.75, $3.25, or $10, you don't "take away" and the outlet does not have to "give up" what's shown on it to complete the transaction (i.e., the price of $2.75, $3.25, or $10).

Be it in barter or otherwise, *price has never been a part of any exchange ever transacted in the human world* (that means any work that is built on or derived from it is not going get anyone anywhere).

Though the kind of surpluses that we trade nowadays are quite different from those that were carried out a few millennia ago, all "priced" exchanges that have ever taken place voluntarily in human societies have one thing in common. Just like barter, each and every single one of them is bilateral. It has *the subject* on the one hand, which can be intangible, and *money* on the other.

There is nothing else for us to consider.

Indeed, price is *neutral* by nature. No one is in the position to claim what price is right in any individual exchange. Low price is certainly good for the buyer, but it's bad to the seller. Conversely, it must be great for the seller but extremely unwelcoming to the buyer if the price is high. Otherwise, it is totally none of our concern—if we're "bystanders."

Many people, however, often find high prices unacceptable (in some cases, why buyers are so badly in need of something yet they can't afford to pay is another question entirely).

Maybe the work of those holier-than-thou scholars should have included one specific human side of economics. People are *possessive* and *selfish*—as they're always prepared to take but reluctant to give.

As sellers, they would naturally wish to "take away" as much as they could from buyers, whereas the latter would do their best to "give up" as little as possible to the former. It is therefore money—*not* price—that truly, truly concerns people the most in their life, where price—as numeric—allows the transacting parties to know exactly *how much to pay or to receive* when the exchange is completed (where an amount of money is passed from the payee to the payer).

That's all.

There are tens of millions if not billions of transactions taking place around the globe every day. *Each is a unique affair that bears no relationship whatsoever with any other.* Your decision to enjoy a cup of coffee at the Starbucks store certainly will have no repercussion on the exchanges to be carried out by your neighbors or colleagues.

This is common sense.

Henceforth, no one needs to know anything about what's to be transacted by others—unless he or she intends to "undo" what have already been honored by the rest.

Interestingly, economists are able to use the figure shown above to aggregate all the markets to form an "economy" that has a price level and an output level as well for them to research, write, publish, and advise governments on how to manage and control the economic well-being of their country.

In the rarefied circle of top economists, the so-called economic management is the main battlefield fought between Keynesians, the followers of John Maynard Keynes (1883–1946), and *monetarism.* The latter is pioneered by Milton Friedman (1912–2006).

Whichever school they're affiliated to, this group of scholars always have two key concerns in the study of macroeconomics, which is based on a set of equations developed by Keynes (to be shown in chapter 7). One is about *inflation* and the other is related to *economic growth.* The former refers to rising prices, which, in their eyes, is a "monster."

In truth, inflation is never an issue if it is about prices. Logically speaking, between the creation of money and high prices, one of them must take place first. Once the cause occurs, we can just ignore the effect—as no price, low or high, *will ever cause anything else in the world to change.*

As for the latter, it is to be measured, according to economists, by what is "produced" by us. Given that the production of output—which has physical substance—depends on what nature has to offer while humans have endless needs and desires to be satisfied, ultimately there is an issue for all of us to ponder. *What will eventually happen to the planet when humankind are relentless in their pursuance of economic growth?*

Let us first explore the only truly universal language among humans—irrespective of nationalities, races, cultures, or religions.

It "drives" the world.

2

IMAGINARY AND REAL

The key role of money, as we saw in the previous chapter, is to facilitate human exchanges. People have been using it for thousands of years. No one ever had or has any difficulty understanding exactly what it is. Money is just an object that *marvelously allows us to get whatever we want.*

It's that simple.

But to a group of scholars who may receive an attractive prize to be awarded by the Bank of Sweden—if their works are considered to be outstanding and exceptional by Nobel Prize selection committee— money is more than just a medium of exchange. It is also a store of value, a unit of account, and a standard of deferred payment as well.

And that's not all. Instead of highlighting its uniqueness as the only common denominator in *all* monetary exchanges or transactions, they treat money as though it is a "commodity."

As the most popular and famous economist, John Maynard Keynes published a book in two volumes titled *A Treatise on Money* in 1930. In the book, Keynes said that people have "demand" for money owing to three motives. The first is for conducting exchanges, and it is known as the *transactional motive.* Second, people have to hold money in case of emergencies, as they may need it urgently. This is the *precautionary motive*. Last, people hold money because they can easily switch it to other types of assets. When people are torn between choosing to hold money and other assets, the psychological torment will become the *speculative motive* in holding money.

In monetary theories, the last motive is far more important than the other two.

According to Keynes's model, people in their life always have two things to hold: money and the proxy for all other tradable assets, i.e., bonds. The latter are issued by firms to fund their investment. In return, the issuers will pay a fixed amount of interest periodically to the bearers until the terms of the bonds expire. Hence, when bond prices increase, interest rates fall, while interest rates will rise when the bond prices decrease.

In sum, interest rates and bond prices are *negatively* related.

Here is how interest rates are linked to our demand for money. When the former is high, bond prices would be low. People in this case would rush to buy bonds, hoping their prices would soar in the near future. Given that they have to pay for the bonds bought, their demand for money would fall. Conversely, when interest rates are low, people would not wish to hold bonds (since their prices are high). They hold money. Based on the *negative* relationship between the rates of interest and the collective amount of money demanded by all the people living in the economy—via the so-called speculative motive—economists will plot the demand-for-money curve as downward-sloping.

It looks like Keynes must have contributed almost half of the monetary principles found in modern economics.

In *A Treatise on Money*, Keynes also proposed that the central bank should be given the "unchallengeable power in controlling the volume of bank-money,"[2] as any event "which tended to influence the behavior of the majority of banks in the same direction whether backward or forward, would meet with no resistance and would be capable of setting up a violent movement of the whole system."[3]

As the father of Keynesianism, Keynes obviously believed that the central bank could have the power to regulate the amount of money circulating in the economy. However, it was Milton Friedman who proudly included three specific monetary instruments in one of his reputable works for the central bank to control the "supply" of money.

According to Friedman, the amount of money to be circulating in any banking system depends on two elements: *money multiplier* and *high-powered money*. The former contains two ratios. To illustrate the first, let's say a man deposits $1,000 in a bank. As the normal practice, the bank manager has to set aside a *reserve*. If the amount is $200, then the so-called deposit-reserve ratio (DRR) is 20 percent.

After setting aside this amount of reserve, the bank manager can lend out the remaining $800. This amount of loan will become the deposit of another bank, which will be in a position to lend $640 after setting aside $160 as a reserve, and such a process of "deposit creates loan, and loan creates deposit" will go on indefinitely.

To capture the last cent and the last bank in this endless process, Friedman applied the knowledge of mathematics. By taking the reciprocal of the deposit-reserve ratio, i.e., 1/DRR, the multiplying process stops.

In the aforementioned illustration, $5,000 of deposits could be created in the banking system, as the deposit-reserve ratio is 20 percent and the initial deposit is $1,000.

Given that the ratio has a multiplying impact on the sum of money to be generated in the banking system, Friedman suggested that the central bank should make it mandatory for all the banks under its supervision to adhere to a declared rate. Once the banks obey the directive, the ratio will become the first of the three monetary instruments mentioned, termed the *required reserve ratio* (RRR). The reciprocal of this ratio will produce a value for the money multiplier, which could be 5, 10, or more, depending on the RRR set by the central bank.

This is the first of the two ratios contained in the money multiplier. In theory, the central bank would not set a required reserve ratio as 100 percent, as the value of the money multiplier is only 1. It should not set the ratio at 0 percent either, as the money supply will become "infinity." Otherwise, between these two numbers, the ratio must be quite an effective instrument for the central bank to multiply the money supply of its economy, except that he raised a concern. Friedman believed *bills* formed a part of the reserves—where withdrawals would cause "leakages." He then included the second ratio, i.e., deposit-currency ratio (DCR), in the multiplier.

And so, as long as all ordinary citizens fully understand the possible downside of "leakages" and keep the number of bills in their wallets as few as possible, then the DCR would have a minimal impact on the money supply. That is to say if the RRR is set to be 20 or 10 percent, the value of the money multiplier will not be too far below 5 or 10, respectively.

From here on, the central bank would have two tools to control the amount of high-powered money. The first is called *open-market operation.*

In Friedman's definition, high-powered money is the amount of deposits banks hold in the books of the central bank. Whenever the latter sells or buys securities, the amount of deposits held by the former in their books will fall or rise, respectively. It will in turn cause the money supply to change (with a multiple amount).

The other instrument is *discount rate*, which acts like a "cost" of borrowing to banks. If the central bank would want to lower it, banks will knock on its window for borrowing "cheap" money. Should the central bank raise the discount rate, all the banks should get the hint. Thus money supply will change whenever the central bank adjusts the discount rate (again, the effect is multiplefold).

Since Friedman and his protégés believe these three monetary instruments are sufficient to render the central bank with the absolute power to control the amount of money circulating in the economy, they will plot the money-supply curve in a straight line upward, or vertically—for them to shift—where banks "intermediate" between depositors and borrowers, i.e., to accept the money of the former so that they could lend it to the latter.

One group of economists, however, takes a completely different approach. They plot the money-supply curve horizontally. To them, banks will supply money for people and organizations to meet their transactional motive. That means the circulating amount of money will depend on the level of economic activities. In their model, the flat-looking supply curve is the *interest rate*, which supposedly shows how saving and investment could dictate our future prosperity, so the central bank could shift it up or down to manipulate ordinary citizens "to hold between money and other assets" (i.e., via the speculative motive).

They are post-Keynesians.

The key difference between these two distinct versions of money supply is that one school holds that money is the *cause* while the other believes it is the *effect*.

Such a disagreement in causation will generate two scenarios.

The so-called money market has three curves, where one is nicely sloping downward, the other is sloping upward, and one more is going side-ways.

Otherwise, there are two money markets for us to plot. Both have a demand curve sloping from left to right, but one of them has a vertical money-supply curve whereas the other has a horizontal one.

Unless someone is able to prove that the three curves of the first case will always intersect at precisely the same spot, and in the second case, the two equilibrium points of the two diagrams will be producing an identical outcome in the real world, the works from these two schools of monetary thought will naturally produce what exactly Friedman wished to show us.

To the economist who believed the central bank possesses the power to multiply the money supply on the one hand while "trying hard" to control it on the other, money has two quantities. One is *nominal*, which is defined by Friedman as "the quantity expressed in whatever units are used to designate money."[4] Or this is just an amount of money that is circulating in the economy at any given time.

On nominal quantity, Friedman often sang, "One man can reduce his nominal money balances only by persuading someone else to increase his. The community as a whole cannot in general spend more than it receives; it is playing a game of musical chairs."[5] The chorus of his tune was "One man's spending is another man's receipts."[6]

The last statement clearly implies that the price of the subject in any individual exchange, which could be an asset, bonds, a painting by Vincent van Gough, a bottle of Château red wine, or anything else, must be absolutely immaterial in the nominal quantity.

To grasp the second or the other quantity of money envisioned by Friedman, let's assume the Federal Reserve of the United States decreases the discount rate to increase an amount of nominal money in the nation. When they have more money, the 325 million Americans would "seek to dispose of what they regard as their excess money balances by paying out a larger sum for the purchase of securities, goods and services, the repayment of debts, and as gifts."[7] Once people are prepared to pay out and "give away" more, prices should be rising. And so, if the nominal quantity increases faster than the rise in the price level, then the output level in the economy will also increase. Conversely, if the nominal quantity increases slower than the rise in prices, then the output level of the US economy would shrink. But if Americans are able to foretell that the increase in the nominal amount of money will be fully offset by the rise in prices (i.e., there are no changes in the so-called *real* money, defined by Friedman as "the quantity expressed in terms of the volume of goods and services the money will purchase"[8]), then there will be no change in the output level of the country.

This is how an economy functioned in the mind of Friedman. It all depends on what happens when we take the nominal quantity divided by a price level—which is irrelevant in our daily transactions —to get this: if the "real" money rises or falls, so does the output level, respectively. For his ability to distinguish any sum of money in *two* entirely different quantities, Milton Friedman is considered to be one of the two most authoritative and influential economists of the past century (the other is John Maynard Keynes).

In the human world, no one will ever demand lesser amounts of money for any motive (even a fifth grader is fully aware that if having some money is good, then having more of it must be better).

Likewise, it is impossible for any banking system to generate a multiple amount of money supply, yet no one notices it.

As a novelist and Harvard professor of economics who favored big and powerful government to run the country, John Kenneth Galbraith (1908–2006) once said that money was "the most magically alluring subject of economics"[9] and that no one "knew with certainty what, in the modern economy, is money."[10]

At any given moment in time, the world does have an amount of money circulating *for all global citizens to pay one another for anything* (they surely know where to exchange their foreign monetary units, if they do not get their payments in local currencies).

It is always *real* (i.e., that is to say it has nothing to do with our imagination).

3

WHENCE IT CAME

In the old days, money was in physical form. In the modern world, payments can easily be wired electronically—where physical money is mostly sought after by museums and collectors. Yet Karl Brunner (1916–1989), as one of the founders of monetarism, still considers money to be best defined "in the classical tradition to refer to any object generally accepted and used as a medium of exchange,"[11] where the *object* could be seashells, salt bars, silver, or gold.

Obviously the form of the object wasn't an issue. Any tangible object accepted by people living in primitive societies to transact for anything was money.

That is to say *general acceptability* was key.

In the history of the development of physical money, silver had the longest run. It was passed as bullion by weight in ancient Mesopotamia in the Middle East and Egypt as early as the third millennium BC. The standard weights, which only the king had the authority to declare, were *mina* (weighted less than a pound) and *shekels* (a sixth of a *mina*). People, however, slowly realized that carrying bullion with them to trade was highly inefficient and cumbersome. They always had to diligently weigh and cautiously assay its value. For this reason, they started to use coinage—bullion made of predetermined weight—to transact exchanges.

According to Jonathan Williams et al., the first coins in the Western tradition were minted in the kingdom of Lydia in western Asia Minor as far back as the sixth century BC.[12] These coins were in specie—full-weight coins made of pure bullion. In ancient Greece, Athens and Corinth were the first Greek city-states to mint their own coins, which were mainly in silver, during the fifth century BC.

Unlike Lydian coins, these coins were *in tale*—i.e., their content was *less than* their face value. (If there are coins in specie, i.e., with no divergence between their face values and substances, still lying somewhere on earth at this moment, it must be that their owners didn't bring them along with them when knocking on the door of heaven or hell. As they say, "You can't take it with you.")

Today we may find these two types of coins in museums; back then it was coins *in tale* that experienced exciting development.

In about AD 800, Charlemagne (742–814), king of the Franks and emperor of the Holy Roman Empire, decreed that a pound of silver be struck into 20 *shillings*, while each shilling referred to 12 *pennies*, so that a pound of silver could be struck into a total of 240 pennies. He then imposed this type of monetary system on the territories he conquered, where such a conversion rate was later developed into the Carolingian system of pounds, shillings, and pence found throughout the continent of Europe.

During the long period of time when coins *in tale* were used as money, clever (or we should say unscrupulous) people knew how to come up with various creative and innovative means to exploit the intrinsic value of money. They used short weighting, clipping, and counterfeiting to swindle their unsuspecting trading partners. People therefore often found that whenever lower-valued coins were circulating in the market, higher-valued coins would disappear. Sir Thomas Gresham (1519–1579), the founder of the Royal Exchange and financial adviser to Queen Elizabeth I, had a simple phrase to describe the monetary phenomenon: *bad money drives out good.*

As a matter of fact, the exploitation of the value of coins wasn't confined to private initiatives. Together with their subjects, queens, kings, and other rulers could use three tools to cheat as well. They reduced coins' weight, reduced their fineness (by increasing the amount of nonprecious alloy), and simply reduced their value by decree (this is what we call "devaluation" in modern world). The activities of the clippers and forgers, plus the decrees of rulers and states, produced a series of cycles of debasement and reform of coins.

In Europe, silver coinage was debased to 1,680 pennies in the year 1500. By 1700, a pound of silver was debased to be worth 3,192 pennies.

The Carolingian system, mentioned in one of John F. Chown's works, eventually "had survived the ravages of depreciation only in England and, rather less successfully, in Scotland; in the rest of Europe the system had disappeared in terms of actual coins."[13]

And probably owing to the use of physical money being highly hazardous, the system could not last up to a millennium. Besides their having to stay vigilant in order not to be shortchanged, people found physical money—be it in bullion or coin in specie or *in tale*—was inconvenient and risky to bring along with them to trade (or keep at home). They therefore had another kind of "need."

As early as the fourth century BC, a new institution emerged in Athens that specialized in the safekeeping of bullion and coins for people, including traders: banks.

According to John Kenneth Galbraith, who believed money was a magically alluring subject of the discipline that he preached, banks "had a substantial existence in Roman times, then declined during the Middle Ages as trade became more hazardous and lending came into conflict with the religious objection to usury."[14]

The last was indeed considered by the renowned ancient Greek philosopher Aristotle (384–322 BC) to be the most hated sort of moneymaking, stating that usury was money bred of money "as offspring resemble their parents."[15]

Banks, however, were prominent in several cities in Italy when trade revived and flourished during the thirteenth century. Owing to their intimate association with trade, Bologna, Florence, Genoa, Pisa, and Venice were serious challengers as banking centers. With their relatively dense populations dominated by merchants with immerse wealth, these cities became independent city-states.

To Galbraith, banking, as the recognized precursors of modern commercial banks and as businesses with ethnic association, "belongs to the Italians."[16]

When banks, Italian or otherwise, accumulated precious coins in their vaults (for convenience, we shall ignore bullion), some curious scholars began to theorize about what was done with them. Banks could always lend part of the deposited coins to borrowers, since the chance of all depositors withdrawing their coins at once was extremely slim. But they had to keep part of the deposited coins in their vaults as *reserves* in case of withdrawals. Once coins were used by banks to meet the needs of borrowers, the end amounts would be a few times more than the original ones. Such a belief became what are known as the concepts of *intermediation* and *money multiplier* that are found in the study of modern economics.

If people loved their money so much that they didn't mind paying the banks to keep it safe, there is no reason to suspect that the depositors were totally unaware of it when the valuable coins they'd placed with the bank had been lent to some strangers without their knowledge.

Besides, no person would pay to borrow coins from one bank and then pay again to another bank for storing them in the vault, given that the borrower already had the "perfect" opportunity of running away with the most valuable metals in their societies.

As a matter of fact, even if banks really did "intermediate" in those days, which definitely had to be carried out surreptitiously without arousing the interest of some imaginative scholars, it was impossible for any bank to use what was subject to *physical availability* to generate a "multiple" amount of coins, physically speaking.

Bankers were no magicians.

Initially, the role of banks was to keep the money of others safe. When people demanded the service, *bills* would be issued by banks for certifying the quantity and the type of coins deposited, where later depositors could present them for withdrawal. In the books, these transactions would be recorded as "in" and "out" in an account bearing the name of the depositor. The balance in each of the accounts would then show the ought-to-be physical quantity of the coins that should be in the vault of the bank—unless burglary or embezzlement caused a discrepancy.

Gradually, people found it more convenient to endorse and pass around the bills issued by banks or just write another bill with instructions to transfer a specific amount of coins to a named party, instead of every now and then going to the banks to withdraw and deposit the coins. After all, this was the factor of why banks were set up in the first place, except they had to ensure that all the endorsements were genuine when bills were presented by people for withdrawals—given that it was not the original depositor who asked to withdraw the coins.

When that happened, two developments followed. One was trivial. The in-and-out recording system became obsolete. Banks had to record two entries in two accounts (which became the basis of what's known as the double-entry principle of today), as the owners of coins had to be transferred. If the transaction involved two banks, they would hold an account vis-à-vis each other and settle the transfer of physical coins later.[17]

The other development, however, completely transformed the role of banks.

These institutions, which were at first established to keep people's coins safe, soon realized that they were in the position to issue bills *without the backing of anything*, and, unsurprisingly, they seized the opportunity.

And for one simple reason, people were quite happy to accept the bills issued by banks as payments in their transactions. Unlike physical coins, which required people to always vigorously assay their value, paper bills, which had denominations in *numbers* that were simple and easy for transacting parties to understand, were extremely convenient in trade. Hence, people didn't mind paying *interest* to banks instead of paying "physical money" to keep their coins—i.e., money—safe.

In his book *An Enquiry into the Nature and Effects of the Paper Credit in Great Britain*, Henry Thornton (1760–1815) wrote a short but vivid description of why people would accept bills, which were nothing more than paper with written or printed numbers, issued by banks so readily. He noticed that when "confidence rises to a certain height in a country, it occurs to some persons that profit may be obtained by issuing notes, which purport to be exchangeable for money"[18] and "the circulation of a bank note is owing rather to the circumstance of the name of the issuer being so well known as to give to it an universal credit."[19]

In short, confidence or faith "is the foundation of paper credit."[20]

Banks in those days must have been apt to distinguish the two types of bills they issued. One entitled the rightful owners with the ability to withdraw their deposited coins.

As for the other type of bills, the holders obviously had no such entitlement, but Thornton claimed that they were purported "to be exchangeable for money."

Such an ambiguity about exchangeability from paper bills to physical coins, paradoxically, led many governments in the West to establish *convertibility*.

The monetary system involved three parties.

There was a group of ordinary people who assumed something to be true. The second was a group of bankers who preferred to keep quiet and not to disclose to others what they had done in their books. Last but not least, there was a government that behaved as if it knew everything—except that the bills issued by banks were created by nothing but *book entries*.

How we wish we lived in the era when we could exchange paper bills for something "solid."

In a country where the Carolingian monetary system survived, convertibility was put to a test in 1797 when rumors of a French invasion caused the public in England, which generally didn't have coins deposited at any bank, to rush to the Bank of England for conversion with their bills.

When many people from all walks of life were found lining up outside the bank anxiously demanding the institution to turn their "convertible" bills into something else, Parliament reacted by ordering the bank to stop exchanging.

This must be the only logical and practical action available for the authority to tackle the crisis.

No government could ever fulfill its promise to exchange bills for coins.

In 1931, the British government finally made the wise decision to abandon the gold standard (that meant people living in the country could no longer use their "pound" to exchange for gold, which was more valuable than silver).

Across the ocean where Christopher Columbus sailed, the monetary system that needed the government to make an insane promise lasted from 1879 until 1971—the year when the Vietnam War and America's troubling domestic economic issues led President Richard Nixon to officially declare its suspension.

Ever since then, convertibility has simply become a historical term, a relic of a bygone era.

The transformation of money from physical forms to its current being, i.e., something penned in the books of banks, had already taken place a long, long time ago. Exactly when the process was completed is beyond the scope of this book, the focus of which is to unveil what's unfound in economics.

4

A Big, Big Zero

As an object that everyone intrinsically recognizes, money must be the most sought-after object by humankind.

In modern days, banks are the only institutions that allow us to withdraw bills, which are often printed solely by governments. The exception is rare. In the United Kingdom and the last colony it gave up, in 1997, Hong Kong, banks are still allowed to print their own bills. In any case, withdrawals will cause the bills held by nonbank parties—i.e., people and organizations—to increase while the amount of account balances penned in the books of banks to decrease by the *exact* same value.

The reverse will hold true when bills are deposited at the counters of banks.

To meet the demand for bills by the public, banks have to determine a *fraction* somewhere between zero and the full sum of account balances penned in their books that can't be set too low.

Imagine what people would do when told by their bank that there were no bills for them to withdraw.

It must be a tough job for bankers, given that they have to strike a delicate balance between holding too many and not holding a sufficient amount of bills.

Given that withdrawals and deposits will all have records in the books of banks, there are *no* dreaded leakages. If it does, some bills must have already been physically destroyed or lost forever owing to the stupidity or negligence of a select few.

People can choose between holding bills and account balances, but they just can't have more of one without giving up the other. No one needs to dwell on this, except: between the two, account balances must be penned in the books of a bank first before any withdrawal—unless these financial institutions grant overdraft to some parties or someone has a plan to rob a bank or to dig a tunnel leading to its vault.

Our money must be originated from the books of banks.

To illustrate, let's assume Bank X in Country A buys a car at $25,000 from Car Inc. for the chief executive officer, while approving a loan for Tom to purchase a car of the same model from the same firm at the same price. These transactions will be reflected in its books as such:

Bank X ($)

Car	25,000	Car Inc.	50,000
Loan to Tom	25,000		

This is how account balances, as money, are created.

It is based on the principle of *double entry*, which states that for any transaction there is a debit entry and a credit entry to be recorded in two accounts.

Any banker or accountant can verify the illustration.

Once credited to its account, Car Inc. can turn some of the $50,000 into bills while making payments to others. To illustrate how banks' liabilities flow freely from one's books to another's, assume Car Inc. pays Dick $5,000, whereupon the latter places the check in Bank Y.

The transaction will cause the books of the two banks to have these entries:

Bank X ($)			
		Car Inc.	(5,000)
		Bank Y	5,000

Bank Y ($)			
Bank X	5,000	Dick	5,000

This payment will cause a sum of account balances to be transferred from Car Inc.'s account held in the books of Bank X to Dick's account found in the books of Bank Y.

The accounts these two banks hold vis-à-vis each other can be referred to as *interbank accounts*, which will "vanish" once we combine their books. The credit balance of $5,000 in the books of Bank X will be fully offset by an exact debit balance of $5,000 in the books of Bank Y, where the total amount of money circulating in Country A remains as $50,000 (the sum of $45,000 and $5,000 in the accounts of Car Inc. and Dick, respectively).

This point still holds true in cases where bank liabilities flow across national boundaries. For instance, Bank Y asks all the banks in Country B, where its monetary unit is the pound sterling, to quote an exchange rate between dollar and pound for Dick, who wants to give away £2,500 to Harry, who lives in Country B. And it turns out that Bank Z quotes the best rate: $1 to £1 (that means the rest of the banks in Country B ask for more than one dollar to exchange for one pound). As a profit-seeking institution, Bank Y sells the pounds to Dick at the rate of $1.01 and charges him $5 for issuing the bank draft. In its books, which are denominated in dollars, these are the entries:

Bank Y ($)		
	Equities	30
	Dick	(2,530)
	Bank Z ($1 : £1)	2,500

Bank Y enjoys an income of $30, of which $25 is the spread between buying low and selling high in the foreign-exchange transaction, something Bank Z can earn too. If it buys the dollars from Harry at the rate of $1 to £0.99 and charges him £5 for the bank service, then in the books of Bank Z, which are denominated in pounds, will have these entries:

Bank Z (£)

Bank Y ($1 : £1)	2,500	Equities	30
		Dick	2,470

The bank now holds a debit balance of $2,500 in the interbank accounts vis-à-vis Bank Y for the pounds it sold at $1 to £1, while earning £30 of revenue.

Should Harry prefer to receive the "gift" in dollars, then the interbank account balances of Bank Y and Bank Z, though from two banking systems, will be an identical offsetting amount in dollars.

When this kind of situation occurs, then Bank Z is said to hold Eurodollars. That is, if an American bank holds pesos as assets as well as liabilities in its books, it is said to hold euro-pesos, which can flow from the books of a foreign bank. Or the bank can just create them by double entries—as long as the governments of both countries have no objection. Hence, the term *Eurocurrency* is not confined to foreign monetary units held by European banks, though the most popular type of Eurocurrency is, nonetheless, the Eurodollar.[21]

In any case, Bank Z holds $2,500 of assets that are the liabilities of Bank Y—irrespective of the rate of exchange agreed between them. In other words, we may reset the exchange rate in the illustration, say having $1 to exchange for £10 or £1 to get $100, Bank Y still "owes" Bank Z the same amount of $2,500. Should a different exchange rate be used, the only effect is on the books of Bank Z. Harry will have a different amount of account balances that are fully backed by the exact same amount of assets penned in the books of Bank Z for the $2,500 of liabilities flowed from the books of Bank Y.

Just like the banks within the same system, once we stack the books of Bank Y and Bank Z, their interbank accounts, which have $2,500 of debit balances and $2,500 of credit balances at the same time, will fully offset each other and disappear.

Now let's assume Bank X depreciates 20 percent of the car it bought for its CEO and Tom has $2,500 in his account to repay 10 percent of his loan. The depreciation of the car and the repayment of the loan will cause the books of Bank X to have these entries:

Bank X ($)

| Car | (5,000) | Equities | (5,000) |
| Loan to Tom | (2,500) | Tom | (2,500) |

This is how money is destroyed by book entries. It occurs when a bank writes off its assets and liabilities simultaneously in its books.

Every set of books is kept entirely based on the principle of double entry. We can therefore "aggregate" the books of all the banks across the globe to get this:

GLOBAL BANKING SYSTEM

Physical Assets	Equities
Financial Assets	Financial Liabilities
Bills Held	Account Balances
	Bills Issued
TOTAL ASSETS	**TOTAL LIABILITIES**

This two-sided statement, which includes the books of commercial banks, investment banks, merchant banks, offshore banks, local and regional central banks, the IMF, the World Bank, etc., is derived from the *accounting equation*, which is shown at the bottom.

The statement must have a beginning in human societies, when people began to accept bills issued by banks as money.

Though it contains no concrete figures, the statement must have captured all the transactions that have taken place in the books of all the banks up to this point and will continue to do so from this moment onward until, alas, the end of civilization. It would be with us all the time—no matter what has happened to the world, be there outbreaks of pandemics, natural disasters, social unrest, crashes in stock markets, financial and political turmoil, inflation, depression, war—unless, that is, we decide to revert to barter or use physical money. Otherwise, there has been a big, big "zero" overseeing all human endeavors since its inception.

The number is derived from the *difference* between the two sides of the accounting equation produced by the statement (i.e., total assets = total liabilities).

No interbank account will ever appear in the statement, as all of them—irrespective of the exchange rates agreed between two banks that are denominated in two different monetary units—will fully offset each other, *pair by pair*.

The total assets in the statement consist of *physical assets*—which are self-explanatory, *financial assets*—which are usually made up by bank loans and what's invested in the stocks and bonds issued by other nonbank organizations—and *bills held*. The last refers to the amount of bills issued by central banks that is still lying in the vaults of banks. It will not appear if all the banks in the world are allowed to print their own bills.

On its right, the total liabilities have four components, of which *account balances* is the largest. It is the "amount of money" that is available for nonbank parties to consume, to invest, to save, to pay, or to "give away." When they purchase the stocks and the bonds issued by banks, then their account balances will be transferred to the other two components, namely *equities* and *financial liabilities*, respectively (no one bank in modern days will ever assay and accept bullions or coins for capital contribution). Or they can save by turning their account balances into time deposits, which will cause the financial liabilities of banks to rise. As for the last component, i.e., *bills issued*, it has two parts. One is the amount of bills issued by central banks to their banks, while the other is the amount of bills withdrawn from the books of those banks that are allowed to print their own bills.

Whether the bills are printed by the central bank or banks, we all know that withdrawals and deposits will never ever cause the amount of money circulating in the world to change—as bills and account balances are the "perfect substitutes" for each other.

Here are the few points that we could learn from this simple statement that is based on what's practiced universally by all qualified accountants, i.e., the accounting equation.

Banks *do not* intermediate, i.e., to accept the money of the public and lend it to others. "Deposits" is an outdated term. We live in the Space Age, where payments can be made by paper, such as by check, or electronically.

Indeed, all the terms demonstrated by Milton Friedman in his concept of money supply *are totally absent in the books of banks.* There are no "leakages," no reserves, no deposits (but account balances), no high-powered money, and certainly there is no "money multiplier"—as he himself already made it clear that his spending must be someone else's receipts.

Second, it is only when a bank pens an asset and credits the account of a nonbank party or writes off an asset by decreasing the same amount of its liabilities at the same time, then there will be a change in the size of the big, big zero. Otherwise, all transactions between banks and nonbank parties—whether the payments are made by the former and received by the latter or vice versa for anything, including interest—*will only cause the composition of the liabilities in the statement to change.*

The conclusion also covers foreign-exchange transactions. For instance, Harry wishes to return the "gift" mentioned in a previous illustration to Dick, and the exchange rate has become $1 to £1.01. After charging Harry £5 for the banking service, the following will be the entries in the books of Bank Z:

Bank Z (£)

Bank Y ($1 : £1)	(2,500)	Equities	30
		Harry	(2,530)

Harry needs £2,525 to exchange for $2,500 owing to the appreciation of the dollar, which will let Bank Z gain £25 from the foreign-exchange transaction and £5 of bank charges.

In the event that the dollar depreciates to $1 to £0.99 when Harry wants to "give back" the money, then the outcome will be the exact reverse of the above. These are the entries in the books of Bank Z (with £5 of bank charges):

Bank Z (£)

Bank Y ($1 : £1)	(2,500)	Equities	(20)
		Harry	(2,480)

Bank Z will suffer a loss of £25 on the foreign-exchange transaction, as it can only deduct £2,475 from Harry, while the $2,500 flows back to the books of Bank Y. Its loss, however, is reduced to £20 because of the banking service it provided for Harry.

Appreciation of a currency is always good for banks that hold it but it is bad for nonbank parties, and vice versa in the case of depreciation.

Since *fluctuation in interest rates or exchange rates will not cause the amount of total assets or total liabilities penned in the books of all the banks around the globe to change*, we shall conclude that any study related to them—just like price—will lead us to nowhere.

Third, all transactions taking place among banks will have no impact whatsoever on the world. The profit or income earned by one bank will be fully offset by the loss or expense incurred by another. They will therefore be neutralized in one of the seven terms found in the big, big zero (i.e., equities).

The observation also holds for all the transactions between the central bank and its banks, whether it is for the conduct of so-called open-market operation, interest paid (or received), or any other thing. That means the three monetary instruments mentioned by the father of monetarism for the central bank to control the money supply, in the global banking system, *are totally devoid of money* (unless the central bank hands out bills directly to the public).

Last but not least, for every dollar possessed by people and organizations there must be an exact dollar of bank liabilities (a hundred for a hundred, a thousand for a thousand, a million for a million, etc.). Money will therefore vanish from the perspective of aggregate (or in a financial sense). That's why the world has a big, big "zero" overseeing every one of us. The amount of money circulating in the world can be determined by finding the difference between the total assets and the amount of bills held in the global banking system (the deduction is necessary as the bills lying in the vaults of banks are not money until they are withdrawn).

For a single country or banking system, it can be determined by compiling all the assets penned in the books of its banks, including the central bank (we can't peek at their liabilities, as it's an intrusion of their privacy), and then deduct these items. The first is all the *interbank account balances*, including those held against foreign banks at whatever exchange rates are agreed on (whereby they will have the corresponding entries as liabilities, if one would have the chance to peek at the other half of their books). The next are *Eurocurrencies* and *foreign notes* (as they are not in local currency). The last is the amount of *bills held*, which will become money only when they are withdrawn by the public via account balances.

The result is what we call the *quantity of money* (QOM).

At last we've identified the source of our money and how to determine its precise quantity as well. How much we hold, in the real world, depends solely on one and only one factor: how many assets are acquired and how many of them are disposed of in the books of banks—*nothing else*. The quantity will increase if and only if banks acquire more assets than those disposed of. When banks write off many more assets than what's penned in their books, then, sadly, the QOM will fall. Otherwise, no one transaction will ever cause the size of the big, big zero to change.

No one can "make" money without someone "losing" theirs, and vice versa. For a given QOM, it is always a question of whose accounts or pockets the money is in. This is how we can tell the poor from the rich.

5

BANKING CRISIS

Banks are expedient to humankind. These financial institutions have been constantly creating an object that is used by all of us in our daily transactions. It is therefore vital that liabilities can flow from one bank to another's books without questions. If there is a moment when people are told that they can't receive and make payments freely, they'll become panicky and the entire banking system will face a huge crisis.

In the old days when there was no regulatory legislation passed by the so-called elected governments, the working relationship among banks, as noted by Henry Thornton, rested on *confidence* and *credibility*. Nowadays, bankers only need to have a simple piece of paper. Once issued a license, banks in the same banking system under the auspices of the central bank will just accept the liabilities of one another rather readily. But for their liabilities to flow to some other countries, banks will normally need to get another party, such as Standard & Poor's, to evaluate the creditworthiness of the third party before calling each other's agent bank and accepting each other's liabilities.

Banks will always have to closely monitor something that is beyond their control: *the flows of their liabilities.*

Ideally, the inflows and outflows of liabilities between any pair of banks have the tendency to offset each other. If not, banks with outflows would have to pay other banks for holding their liabilities (as it is risky to hold them). The rate of interest on the credit balances in the interbank accounts is called the *interbank rate*—where a high rate indicates the banks operating in the banking system could have severe imbalances in the flows of their liabilities.

Basically, a bank has three options to avoid annoying other banks with the outflow of its liabilities. It could encourage nonbank parties to turn their account balances to time deposits or issue bonds to attract inflow of liabilities. Second, it could sell the government securities on hand to those banks that hold its liabilities (we'll discuss about how government securities could get into the books of banks in the next chapter). In cases where these measures still can't alleviate the problem, the bank can "knock" on the window of its central bank.

To illustrate how the last option works, let us assume Bank X in Country A approaches its central bank because it faces some difficulty getting other banks to accept its liabilities, and the latter is obliging. The central bank agrees to take over $10,000 of Bank X's liabilities from the books of Bank Y. Once the latter is notified about the agreement, the entries in the books of these three banks would look like this:

Bank X ($)

		Bank Y	(10,000)
		Central Bank	10,000

Bank Y ($)

Bank X	(10,000)		
Central Bank	10,000		

Central Bank ($)

Bank X	10,000	Bank Y	10,000

Every party concerned needs only two book entries to achieve a happy ending. Bank Y now holds $10,000 of assets as an amount of debit balances in its interbank account vis-à-vis the central bank, which is more "credible" than an ordinary bank (i.e., Bank X).

But nothing in the world is free. Bank X has to pay interest to the central bank for holding its liabilities. The rate could just be lower than, higher than, or no different from the interbank rate, whereas the central bank has to pay interest to Bank Y. The rate could well be above, below, or equal to what the central bank gets from Bank X. Thus, if the central bank wished to keep the banking system totally free of any crisis arising from some banks refusing to accept other banks' liabilities, it could always declare an "attractive" rate.

However, the role of *taking over the liabilities in the books of its banks* that is undertaken by the central bank has always been wrongly perceived. Economists give it the nickname the "lender of last resort."

Banks never have to borrow given that they have been applying double entries to generate money even before the first central bank was established.

Indeed, they *do not* possess the one object that they have been creating in their books. Every unit of their liabilities is someone else's money, which will be created whenever banks acquire physical assets, approve loans to nonbank parties, and invest in their stocks or bonds (the first explains why banks often have located their headquarters in their own fabulous buildings).

These financial institutions are always wary of one another's liabilities, especially those originating from the books of foreign banks. If for any reason some nations begin to turn down the bank liabilities of a country, then the world will face a *global banking crisis*. That's when the IMF or the regional central bank may have to step in to take over the liabilities of the banking system that are shunned by other countries.

Such operations, again, are always mistaken. Commentators and scholars often claim that the troubled nation is getting "loans" from the IMF, while newspapers usually report that the "debts" of a certain country have to be rescheduled.

In truth, banks neither *need to borrow* nor *owe*. They create money for people to make payments to one another and then destroy it later. One of the greatest challenges any bank has to face in its operations is not to let its liabilities be refused by any other bank.

Originally, the International Monetary Fund was set up at a summit in Bretton Woods, NH, toward the end of World War II to supervise the fixed-rate regime. Under these guidelines, banks had to convert foreign currencies in the interbank accounts using the official declared rates. The regime collapsed at the end of 1971 when the US government devalued its dollar against the currencies of fourteen major industrial countries while indefinitely suspending so-called convertibility, as we saw at the end of chapter 3. The global banking system had to change from a fixed to a flexible exchange-rate regime all because the United States had huge amounts of trade deficits, capital outflow, and others. Yet, so far no one "foreign" bank ever questions its bank liabilities. Banks from Thailand, Indonesia, and Mexico were not so lucky. When many other nations spurned the liabilities of their banks in the 1990s, the world experienced a global banking crisis, which is often wrongly termed a debt crisis.

The latest victim is the birthplace of economics: Greece.

How ironic. The huge sum of outflow of US bank liabilities has made the dollar to be the most popular or sought-after "international monetary unit." (Maybe people still believe the greenback could one day be used to exchange for gold—as the country was the last to give up convertibility.)

Although the global banking system is currently operating under a flexible-rate regime whereby banks from different countries need not seek permission to set their rates of exchange, there are nations still trying to partially "fix" the exchange-rate regime. Besides having to actively take over the foreign currencies in the books of their banks, these governments also have to enforce what's known as *capital control.*

Since no government is so willing to give up the control of the amount of money circulating in its country, we should now focus on *what* actually causes the exchange rate between a pair of monetary units to fluctuate if it is flexible (or not fixed).

Based on the incident in the early 1970s when the superpower had no choice but to devalue its currency, which caused turbulence in the world, we can easily tell that it has to do with *the direction of the flows in bank liabilities between the two countries.* If many banks in Country A want to buy pounds (it is the same to say "sell" dollars), banks in Country B must find a way to safeguard their own interests. Since banks from different banking systems have no interbank rate to reflect the imbalances, banks in Country B will demand that banks in Country A give up more dollars to exchange for pounds before accepting their liabilities. If banks in Country A agree, then the dollar depreciates or the pound appreciates, depending on your perspective. But uneven flows of liabilities between two banking systems may not be the sole cause in the fluctuation of their exchange rates. Factors such as coups d'état, social unrest, political turmoil, or any negative publicity about a country could still cause its currency to depreciate against foreign monetary units.

Be it in fixed or flexible regimes, banks have to ensure that all loans granted to nonbank parties are repaid, and that physical assets penned in their books have to be depreciated and eventually written off (the only exception is some rare physical assets that could be revalued). If any one of them has insufficient equities for any of the above, then in its books it has to write off the assets by reducing its *external* liabilities. In this case, people and organizations that hold its bonds, time deposits, and account balances will have to write off their hard-earned money, too—unless they are "speedy" enough to turn them into bills.

That's called a run, in the classical sense.

People who miss the chance to withdraw bills will just have to accept the hard fact that the amount of bills stored in the vaults of any bank at all times is only a *fraction* of its external liabilities.

The fear of a bank collapse was indeed so formidable that, as the third president of the United States, Thomas Jefferson (1743–1826) once wrote in a letter, "Banking establishments are to be more feared than standing armies."[22]

But to regulators and many others, *lack of liquidity* is the cause of a banking crisis.

In the late 1990s, the severely depressed American real estate market, which still hadn't recovered from the slump in the early part of the decade, provided American banks with an opportunity. They offered attractive interest rates to lure people to become homeowners.

These banks told these borrowers that higher interest rates would come later, something that might not be a concern if the houses they bought could be sold for a good price.

But bankers were also wary that these loans might have been lent to borrowers who might have difficulty honoring their debts. To better manage the risk (or to reduce it), they sliced these mortgages, which were financial assets penned in their books, and placed them into a type of liability-backed security called collateralized debt obligations (CDOs). Once bundled, these banks could offer them to various groups of potential investors.

As an innovative financial derivative, it turned out that not only were CDOs popular among domestic banks, but also banks from other nations. By acquiring these kinds of financial assets, "foreign" banks could cut the amount of the so-called international monetary units held in their books while enjoying returns.

This is how the lovely financial instrument flowed to the books of foreign banks and went "global."

In 2000 there was an unpleasant incident at home that helped to fuel the popularity of CDOs. In that year, the country experienced a technology bust, otherwise known as the dot-com bubble burst. Because many US citizens were worried about a prolonged economic downturn, the Federal Reserve under Alan Greenspan sharply reduced interest rates and kept them low for several years.

In financial circles, low interest rates are always good for market sentiment for investment.

When the Fed kept interest rates low in the early 2000s, some people used a method known as *leverage*—an old-time strategy that allows someone to invest in $5 million of assets with only $1 million of his own—for them to invest in CDOs (where investment banks, such as Lehman Brothers, were key players).

CDOs would never have become global headline news if the homebuyers encouraged by their banks to buy houses had repaid their loans on time. Sadly, the wishful thinking of American banks at the turn of this century became a nightmare for the entire global banking system.

Starting from the summer of 2007, an overwhelming number of homeowners, sweet-talked into taking out loans offered by their banks, have fallen behind on their repayments. When they default on their mortgages, these banks have to write off their assets, which cause their equities to fall. As for those investors of CDOs, they will never be able to recoup the losses, let alone honor their bank loans. That means investment banks have to suffer, too.

All in all, American banks have already created an immense amount of bank liabilities, or "liquidity," that are everywhere *except* in the accounts of the depressed homebuyers and some investors. Other poor Americans might have to write off their account balances—which are money—if they are uninsured, the central bank is unwilling to assist the mismanaged banks, or both. When that happens, a massive-scale banking crisis is bound to take place.

Just imagine what the scene would or could be if the United States had allowed its loss-making banks to collapse. Many people who might prefer to fight standing armies instead of letting money vanish right in front of their eyes would be hysterical. Banks from all over the world would suddenly realize that the much-sought-after international monetary unit—the dollar—that they held was actually a jinx instead of a blessing.

The financial turmoil that followed was named a "credit crunch."

On October 11, 2008, the *Straits Times* of Singapore reported that the US government, since the crisis began in 2007, had pumped $4 trillion into everything from assisting individual homebuyers to bailing out the American Insurance Group (AIG). In Britain, more than £600 billion had been used to buy stakes in banks, to guarantee bank debts, and to provide "loans" for banks by its central bank. In Europe and Russia, the amounts were €500 billion and more than 1 trillion rubles, respectively. In Japan, at least ¥30 trillion were "injected" into the banking system. The total amount of all the above bailout plans is estimated to be more than $6 trillion.

Whatever terms were used to describe the close-shave event, we're curious about how these governments could tackle the crisis. If they had to print bills amounting to $6 trillion to launch the largest financial bailout plans ever carried out in history, we would all have noticed that a vast area of the forests covering the earth had vanished. But no trees were felled (and no banks "collapsed" owing to broken pillars). The central bank must have applied the principle of double entry to *buy* the dud assets, such as CDOs, mortgages, and other financial derivatives, from all those banks that were financially insolvent.

No banking crisis has ever been caused by "lack" of liquidity.

Banks always have the duty of completing the *banking cycle*, i.e., to destroy the money or liquidity they created, where creation is always easy but where trouble will occur if they have to write off their external liabilities, i.e., "our" money—that is, when it suffers negative equities. Bankers therefore have to be prudent whenever it comes to the acquisition of assets in physical, financial, or any other form and to earn income sufficient to cover all expenses incurred.

In principle, it is never the central banker's duty but rather that of all bankers to ensure that none of their acquired assets is dubious. Once they notice that the central bank could take over almost anything from the books of any financial institution under its wing, banks naturally will become bold and adventurous in their dealings.

According to economists, a driver would always drive cautiously if his sports car has no insurance policy. The story becomes quite different if his roaring machine is insured. They attribute the change in the behavior of the driver to a moral hazard.

That's why American banks are so creative and innovative as well. Sheltered by one of the most powerful institutions in the world, i.e., the Federal Reserve, they somewhat know how to appreciate the beauty of book entries and use them for greedy ends.

The assets of some banks could in fact grow to become so huge that the central bank would do whatever it takes to prevent any of them from collapsing. As the saying goes, "The bank is too big to fail!"

The global banking system must have been supervised by a squad of "firefighters" who somehow got the idea that they could alter the amounts of money circulating in their respective countries at their whim, not knowing that in truth they've often been tricked by some well-suited "arsonists."

Regardless of the size, *every bank has the sole responsibility of taking the banking cycle very, very seriously*. If it fails to do so, then its liabilities, which were created for facilitating human exchanges, will become sources of a banking crisis.

6

THE "FIFTH" AVENUE

In human societies, perhaps not many people are fully aware of the spectacular role performed by the central bank. Not only could it take over the liabilities of those banks under its care, but also it can absorb their worthless assets while subduing chaos and panic. Once it successfully averted a banking crisis, which was caused by banks running negative equities, the central bank could just effortlessly leave those dud assets stuck in its books for as long as time permitted— while waiting patiently for the banks to redeem them later.

Alternatively, it could just write off these assets to incur negative equities in its books.

In either case, no one would ever care about how much the central bank "suffers" when everyone else's concern is not to lose his or her money. As long as it is prepared to ensure that no banks under its supervision have external liabilities to be written off owing to bad decisions made by banks in their acquisition of assets, there must now be some money that was supposedly destroyed but is still pretty much alive in the books of banks. In the case where a bank is allowed to forever shut its doors while its dud assets are still held by the central bank, there must be an "indestructible" amount of money that could go on circulating in the global banking system.

We shall call it *phantom liquidity*—because the bank that created it no longer exists.

Hopefully, such a term could let central bankers, policymakers, legislators, and national leaders recognize the misconception of associating the cost of salvaging a banking crisis with taxpayers' money. When it is finally averted with the assistance of the central bank, those account holders, or "taxpayers," could become a kind of beneficiary instead of victims.

A banking crisis could therefore well be a blessing if it ends with phantom liquidity.

According to Charles Goodhart, who held a senior post at the Bank of England before being appointed a professor at the London School of Economics, no government-sponsored bank in Europe, such as the Swedish Riksbank (1668) or the Bank of England (1694), was ever intended to undertake discretionary economic management. Its privileged status owed to the financial resources a government could get from the support of such a bank. It could be a state bank, such as the Prussian State Bank, or a private bank, such as the Bank of England.[23]

Since it was not the foresight of the government but rather its "demand" for money that led to *central banking*, we shall see how the central bank has been faithfully discharging its duty in this aspect once it is placed under the control of politicians, who often want to impress their fellow countrymen how capable, if not wise too, they are.

Throughout the work of economists, the central bank has a crucial role in the economy. It is supposed to "supply" an optimal amount of money that could stimulate *economic growth* without fueling *inflation*.

On the latter, Irving S. Friedman (1915–1989), as an economic adviser to the president of the United States between 1964 and 1970 and who held high positions in the IMF and the World Bank, said that inflation was "a universal solvent of organized societies," as it would "attack and erode the fundamentals on which any organized society rests."[24] (His *Inflation: A Worldwide Disaster* is blurbed by management guru Peter F. Drucker as the best book on inflation.)

In another famous book, *The New Inflation: The Collapse of Free Markets*, economist W. David Slawson boldly declares, "The ability of free markets to keep prices down has collapsed. This is the cause of the new inflation—not too much money or too few goods. What is more, free markets will never again be able to keep prices down."[25]

But we've already noted right from the beginning of the book that no price has ever been a part of any individual exchange. It must be futile to define inflation as rising prices. If free markets can't do the job of keeping prices low, we'll explore how the buyers could get the money to feed the "monster," i.e., rising price level.

According to an article published in the *Economist* (June 3–9, 1995), "Borrowed Time," Americans have been living in debt since their country's founding:

> A national debt, thought Alexander Hamilton, could be a national blessing. Two centuries on, New Yorkers are constantly reminded of just how blessed they now are. For the past six years the national debt clock, a vast electronic scoreboard in midtown Manhattan, has been clocking up the size of America's overdraft, second by $10,000 second, day by $860 million day. By the time Seymour Durst, the clock's creator and a New York property developer, died at age eighty-one, the tally had hit almost $4.9 trillion. That, as the clock's sign helpfully points out, amounts to $63,530 for every one of America's families.

This was the figure in the mid-1990s.

On October 10, 2004, *USA Today* reported that the US national debt had hit $473,456 per American family. That was almost 7.5 times the figure of 1995. And the cumulative amount of debt piled up by the country didn't just stop there. When President Obama vowed to get the US economy out of its trouble by signing the stimulus package of $787 billion less than a month after taking office in 2009, we knew that the figure measuring the sum of American national debt on the vast electronic scoreboard in midtown Manhattan would go well above $4.9 trillion. Indeed, information on nationaldebtclocks.org shows that the United States, or the modern superpower, started 2020 with $22 trillion of national debt.

What a remarkable amount of "borrowed time."

It must be a miracle for any individual to live beyond his means for more than, say, a year.

When the US government is able to incur trillions of dollars of national debt for decade after decade, we're curious. How the country is able to finance that kind of extraordinary miracle.

This amount of debt could be expressed on paper only. That is to say the administration has owed all its staff and contractors and makes no payments at all for whatever amount of "borrowed time" or that, as of this moment, the US government has not paid even a single dollar for the national debt.

This method of financing works if and only if all Americans, including congressmen, senators, and well-respected economists who advise the government on how to manage the economy, would be so patriotic as well as magnanimously generous as to be unpaid for decades, while their government is employing staff and procuring goods, such as carriers, submarines, bombers, and nuclear warheads as well as deploying soldiers to fight wars—all for "free."

If the prerequisite of the first approach is too demanding or unrealistic, then we've to consider the government that borrows from its citizens to finance the national debt (where much of it must be owing to the sum of accumulated budget deficit).

Even if the three richest citizens in the country, Jeffrey Preston Bezzos (the founder of Amazon.com), Bill Gates (the founder of Microsoft), and Warren Buffett (one of the most successful investors in the world), with a combined wealth of about $300 billion totally emptied their coffers, their generous contributions would still be drowned in the ocean of their nation's debt or "borrowed time." For practical reasons, we've to consider the third possibility. It is to let the administration that borrows from banks to honor its debts.

Just like the previous case, the top three banks in the country, Bank of America, Citigroup, and J. P. Morgan Chase, may not be so resourceful that they could finance the astronomical sum of national debt incurred by the administration. Because that someday it will be able to find trillions of dollars—the figure should become much higher in the next decade—to repay its national debt must be an "American Dream." The debt is constantly piling up, not to mention doing so with interest.

And so, here is the last. Unless central bankers, policymakers, Noble Prize winners, and national leaders can answer this, one of these scenarios is bound to be true: first, up to this point of time the US administration has not paid the shortfall between the tax revenue and the amount of expenditures; second, there is a group of friendly Americans who don't mind to let their fellow countrymen happily hold an amount of "borrowed time" via budget; third, American banks are always ready to pay on behalf of the government whenever the latter runs out of money; fourth, an alien from another galaxy has been handing down "the most marvelous object on earth" to the blessed American families whenever the country incurs debts; or fifth, American banks and their central bank work independently, i.e., there are no transactions between them.

The last scenario provides a simple illustration of how the "borrowed time" is financed. Imagine that the US government pays a man named Donald, who claims that he loves money the most, $5,000 on top of the trillions of dollars of debt (where the bill has "Treasurer of the United States" printed on it at one corner). He presents the check at a local bank named the Bank of Multiplier. The following entries are recorded in the books of the Federal Reserve and the bank once the check has cleared:

Federal Reserve ($)

Securities	5,000	Bank of Multiplier	5,000

Bank of Multiplier ($)

Federal Reserve	5,000	Donald	5,000

Donald now holds $5,000 of account balances, which are backed by the exact same amount of interbank account balances held by the Bank of Multiplier vis-à-vis the Federal Reserve (which is the so-called high-powered money found in the works of economists).

This is how the administration uses book entries to pay for the accumulated amount of budget deficits.

The government will always have the "fifth" avenue to run any amount of deficit once the bond is forged between the firefighter and politicians. If the sum is huge, here could be a well-kept two-pronged conspiracy. The central bank could sell Treasury bills for covering up the huge deficits under an instrument suggested by Milton Friedman, named open-market operations, while banks could sell these bills to reduce the imbalances in the flows of their liabilities (which was explained in the previous chapter).

Obviously *national debt* must be an inappropriate term to describe "how much is owed by the government." As money, it has already been placed into someone's pocket. Yet politicians love to squabble among themselves over the cap of the size of deficits. So if the so-called debt plan debated furiously among party leaders fails to get through, then the government might have no more money to pay all its contractors as well as staff on the payroll of the administration such as admirals, generals, congressmen, senators, and secretaries as well as the head of state.

No politicians would allow such a situation to take place while they're in office. There's a name for this situation; if they ever hope to cross this threshold, they may rename it. No one dares to jump off the "fiscal cliff"!

While all banks have to write off whatever assets are penned in their books, a large part of the financial assets held by the central bank can be totally exempted from the *second* half of the banking cycle.

Just like phantom liquidity, budget deficit, which is backed by government securities that have been paid by the central bank, could just go on circulating, both inside and outside the country.

Again, not every country in the world is as fortunate as the superpower, which is built, to a large extent, on book entries (or in laymen's term, by printing money). When the deficit of a nation flows to the books of foreign banks and has no sign of flowing back to its country of origin (probably because its people are fond of imported goods, love to travel overseas, and prefer to invest in foreign countries with their "excess" money), then beyond a certain limit foreign banks may stop accepting any more of that country's bank liabilities.

A recent example is the crisis caused by Greece in the Eurozone of the late 2000s and the mid-2010s.

Given that the amount of money created by central banks in collaboration with their governments does not have to be destroyed in the global banking system, it could indefinitely "inflate" the size of the big, big zero. Henceforth, we shall let inflation have a new lease of life with a brand-new definition. It is *an amount of money created by the central bank for satisfying the financial needs of the government that need not be repaid.* If its amount is astronomical (most likely owing to the number of zeros added onto the currency declared by the state), it's then called hyperinflation.

No one should ever dive for cover if he hears the "monster" roar from now on. This is how the government could calculate its rate. Instruct the central bank to open up its books, where two sums should always be present: A and B. Each is obtained from one side of its books. Sum A is the total of three kinds of *liabilities*: the amount of bills issued (that means banks under its supervision are not allowed to print bills); the amount of Treasury bills issued (which could be used to disguise the real amount of deficits); and the total amount of its interbank account balances vis-à-vis all other banks, including local banks, foreign banks, the regional central bank, and the IMF.

Such a sum will show the amount of liabilities that were created by the central bank that have flowed to the books of other banks.

As for Sum B, we shall look for only one kind of asset. It is the amount of the interbank account balances it holds vis-à-vis all other banks, including the regional development bank and the World Bank. Sum B is the amount of liabilities created by other banks, but now held as *assets* in the books of the central bank.

Finally, we find the *difference* between A and B; if they are equal, C is nothing. Otherwise, we have two cases to consider. If its value is negative, this means that the central bank owes others less than what all other banks combined owe it, and we can just ignore it. But if C has a positive value, that is an amount of "inflated" money created by the central bank for various causes: first, it is the amount of expenses paid or losses incurred by the central bank that go to the books of other banks; second, it is the amount of dud assets bought over by the central bank that may not have to be redeemed (including phantom liquidity); and third, it is the accumulated sum of budget deficits incurred by the government. For a country that generates inflation, it should divide C by QOM—the quantity of money—and multiply it by 100 percent to get the *rate of inflation* (ROI).

Book entries *do not* lie.

In the context of QOM, inflation is definitely great for all ordinary citizens (if not, the taxes collected would be just sufficient to cover all departmental expenses *or* part of the money belonging to taxpayers is in the government coffers). As a matter of fact, they have been embracing her all the while (but are unaware of it, perhaps). No one should ever accuse the government of "wasting taxpayers' money" when it runs a budget deficit (it's merely a question of *who gets it*). Except when people, including the wealthy, are so used to benefiting from half of the budget (i.e., spending on social welfare, healthcare services, education, Social Security, unemployment benefits or employment incentives, all forms of allowances, grants, subsidies, and research funds, lucrative military and other contracts, etc.), they'll get hooked. Whenever the government attempts to tighten its belt or to tame "inflation," it will get all sorts of antigovernment movements such as street protests, demonstrations, and riots that will lead to social unrest and political uncertainty.

Or, in the worst-case scenario, there is ousting.

No wonder Irving S. Friedman wholeheartedly warned us that inflation is the *universal solvent* of all well-organized societies. The moment the monster is unleashed, that's it. One would have to climb over the dead bodies of many who would protect it from being taken away, which, as we've seen, was a concern of President Thomas Jefferson's.

The power of double entry should always be something for every one of us to reckon with. National leaders, who are shrewd politicians, can utilize it for delivering what is despised by all. It is the monster that has been fed by the "puppet," who is also a firefighter: inflation.

MANAGING A "TERM"

In everyday life, we often hear on air, read in print, or watch on screen by someone commenting on the "health" of our economy. Growing, stagnating, or backtracking, each is taken as some kind of indicator of the future. Recovery is good news, so recession must be bad. At times, we are warned by them that our economy, like an airplane, is heading for a "hard landing" (presumably its nose hits the ground first) or a "soft landing" (it lands on its belly).

Before the publication of *The Purchasing Power of Money, Its Determination, and Relation to Credit, Interest, and Crises* by John Maynard Keynes in 1936, all economists were concerned about the individual markets, such as goods, labor, land, and capital, where they believed prices, wages, rent, and interest rates, respectively, would always move to ensure that each of these markets suffered no surpluses or shortages. Or if one ever did, it would only be temporary, as the automatic adjusting mechanisms—e.g., *prices* for goods, *wages* for labor, *rent* for land, and *interest rates* for capital—should take only months at most to eliminate shortages or clear gluts.

One dark historical incident, however, crushed this belief.

During the Great Depression, which lasted years, countless firms in the Western world went bust, unemployment skyrocketed, and almost all the financial markets plummeted. The event was disastrous to the discipline, for which faith in the forces of supply and demand had always been central. It therefore badly needed a savior to get it out of such an unforgiving embarrassment, and here came the greatest economist of all time.

Essentially, Keynes wanted to refute the idea of equilibrium. In *General Theory*, he claimed that producers in the goods market would often behave as if they were monopolies, and unions in the labor market would always repel the idea of lowering wages. Prices were therefore "sticky," and so were wages. That shows that markets would not attain their states of equilibrium automatically.

When the Western world was plagued by the Great Depression starting in 1929, Keynes analyzed its cause by "aggregating" all the markets. And to make his predecessors look like neophytes, he started with a single entrepreneur who sold finished output to others, and then defined "the income of the entrepreneur as being the excess of the value of his finished output sold during the period over his prime cost."[26] This can be expressed as:

Income = Value of Output – Prime Cost

While value of output is sales, the last term comprises two elements. One is *factor cost* and the other is *user cost*.

In normal business terms, factor cost is just the production cost, whereas user cost is derived from the concept of opportunity cost that was first developed by David Ricardo (1772–1823). He applied it to explain why two countries should trade with each other, while Keynes used it to show how the well-being of an economy depends on what the entire population, which may have a size of hundreds of millions or more than a billion, has to forgo.

Since income is defined as the excess of the value of output over its cost, it should be the *profit* to be earned by the entrepreneur. But to Keynes, "the income of the rest of the community is equal to the entrepreneur's factor cost."[27] That is to say, when the operations of all entrepreneurs are summed up, then the aggregate value of all outputs produced will capture *all costs incurred*, including user cost, factor cost, and whatever cost one names, as well as profits earned.

Based on Keynes's such proposition, the economy can in this case be represented as

Income = Value of Output

This is how Keynes painted something for the whole world to be concerned with. The so-called prime cost in *General Theory* has now disappeared right in front of our eyes, where an "economy" is born.

Once the prime cost was made to vanish, Keynes then claimed the output produced by any entrepreneur "must have been sold either to a consumer or to another entrepreneur."[28] From the perspective of aggregate, income can therefore be partitioned into *consumption* and *investment*. The demarcation of the two terms, according to Keynes, corresponded to "where we draw the line between the consumer and the entrepreneur."[29]

Since *savings* was defined by him as the unspent part of income, here is the set of equations developed by Keynes in his *General Theory*:

Income = Value of Output = Consumption + Investment.

Savings = Income − Consumption

Therefore: Savings = Investment.

The last equation shows the equality of investment and savings, an algebraic result of the first two equations.

With an economy made up by *five* distinct parts, here is what Keynes attempted to warn the world about. When interest rates are at low levels, their next most likely movement is in only one direction: up. People will not want to buy bonds today, as they foresee their prices will fall in the future (recall the inverse relationship existing between interest rates and bond prices that was explained in chapter 2). Savings would therefore be trapped in the pockets of ordinary people, so producers have no liquidity to invest, and the economy would then suffer recession (mild) or depression (severe).

This is the theoretical insight provided by Keynes on how the Western world could have suffered a severe economic slump in his lifetime. It is known as the "liquidity trap," a term coined by Sir John Hicks (1904–1989) in 1937 based on Keynes's idea.[30]

Old ladies who keep or hid their money in the mattress must be far scarier than capitalists and industrialists. They have no idea how too much saving could inflict unimaginable damage to the economic well-being of their country. Keynes therefore would not wait for ordinary citizens to empty their coffers to pull or push the economy out of a slump. He would ask the government to swiftly increase spending, so that a kind "multiple" effect could take place almost instantaneously.

To Keynes, everyone in the economy always has the habit of spending a portion of his income. He named it *marginal propensity to consume* (*mpc*) that had a value—say, 80 percent or 90 percent. By applying the formula for the sum of an infinite geometric progression in algebra, Keynes got what's known as the *investment multiplier*. It is equal to the reciprocal of the difference between 1 and the value of marginal propensity to consume, i.e., $1 \div (1 - mpc)$.

So if our government spends $1,000 and the *mpc* is 0.8, then the value of the investment multiplier is 5. That means the income level of our economy can increase from $1,000 to $5,000.

The effect will be "tenfold" if we set the *mpc* at 90 percent.

Just like the money multiplier found in monetary theories, the concept of investment multiplier should sound too good to be true on its face. Yet no one economist asks anything. They rename it to the income multiplier, incorporate it into the equation that says income is equal to consumption plus investment, and then blend them with the two curves developed by Alfred Marshall for them to "visualize" an economy (note that *income* and *output* are always used by economics professors as though they are the same in their teachings):

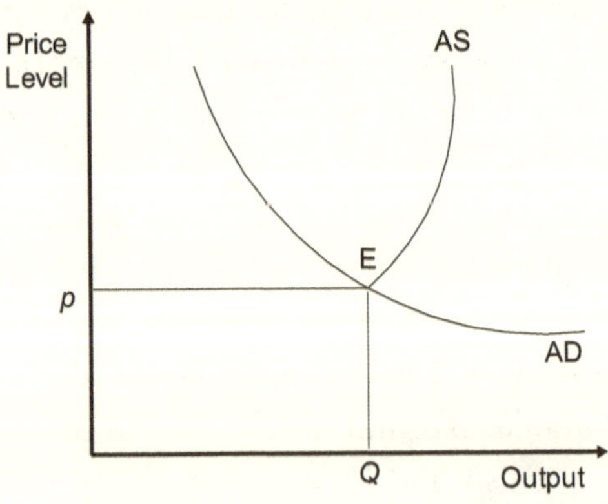

Every economy will have an aggregate demand curve (AD) as well as an aggregate supply curve (AS). The intersection point is marked carefully as E.

The AD curve contains key four components. The first two are actually taken directly from the first in Keynes's set of equation, i.e., consumption and investment. As the third, fiscal policy is always favored by Keynesians, who believe in using "spending" to battle any economic downturn. The last is the difference between the amount of exports and the amount of imports of the country. It is so-called *net exports*, which could be favorable or unfavorable to the economy.

Unlike the AD curve, the AS curve, which has four items too (namely labor supply, labor productivity, capital accumulation, and technology as well), does not slope smoothly but is kinked and has a flat portion. It is owing to the "time frame" defined by Marshall in his *Principles*. In the *short run*, which refers to a time period during which producers can't adjust all their factors of production, the output level of an economy will be constrained by capacity. So, as long as the aggregate demand is not excessive, the AD curve will intersect the part of the AS curve that is flat, so that the overall price level will be stable. It is only when the AD curve moves beyond the maximum productive capacity, i.e., point E, then the AS curve rises steeply, purportedly explaining why prices are rising.

Before the early 1970s, almost all governments in the Western world listened to the followers of Keynes. Based on a curve drawn by William Phillips (1914–1975), i.e., the Phillips curve, this group of scholars maintained that *inflation* and *unemployment* would not occur at the same time. If an economy suffered high unemployment, it should have no inflation. Or if inflation was rampant in the economy, then there would be no unemployment.

In short, they were mutually exclusive.

The world indeed experienced relatively stable price levels for about twenty-five years after World War II. Since inflation was no threat during this period, most Western governments just spent and spent with the hope of attaining full employment (or becoming so-called welfare states).

But good times must end. Starting from the early 1970s, the Western world was plagued by another kind of nasty economic event that challenged Keynesians' thought: *stagflation.*

Unlike the Great Depression, the period of stagflation caused misery to people on both fronts: rising prices and lack of jobs.

It looks like no one should ever touch the AD curve when the economy has a high price level coupled with a low output level. Should someone shift the AD curve to the left, the already low output level worsens. If we shift the AD curve that "hung in the air" to the right, the overall price level goes even higher. Some economists therefore began to focus their attention on the AS curve, and there were governments that believed in this rather novel, if untested, approach to economic management.

In 1979, Margaret Thatcher (1925–2013), better known as the Iron Lady after she became the first woman prime minister of the United Kingdom, tried to undermine the power of unions in the hope of getting more people to join the labor force—because she was told by some advisers that stagflation was caused by rigidity in the labor market, such as powerful unions securing high wages that led to inflation while depriving nonmembers of job opportunities.

Across the Atlantic, the newly elected Reagan administration of the early 1980s tried to rejuvenate the American economy, which had been guided almost solely by Keynes's spirit since the mid-1940s. The US leaders changed the tax structures and loosened regulations as well. These countercyclical measures, according to those economists who proposed them, could motivate people to become more innovative and enterprising, so they could jointly push the AS curve to the right, where stagflation—which in many ways is worse than a depression— could be eliminated "without" doing anything to the AD curve.

This method of managing the economic well-being of a country is named *supply-side economics,* which, unfortunately, does have a huge downside.

In a discipline that tries to portray itself as a branch of science (by writing all sort of equations that can be filled with words, letters, symbols, or combinations of these), it is hard to quantify the real impact of bashing unions or loosening regulations. For this simple reason, most economists will still count on the AD curve to get the economy back on track when it is off the path.

During the early '80s, Milton Friedman triumphantly stole the limelight from Keynesianism, which was humiliated since it'd claimed that inflation and unemployment would exclude each other, before stagflation emerged. When consulted about how to tame inflation while spurring economic growth at the same time, Friedman had a rather simple prescription. He told the government to closely monitor an economic indicator regularly, preferably twice a day, once before bedtime and again first thing in the morning. It should not let the *monetary aggregates*—to be measured by various types of liabilities penned in the books of banks—move beyond the targets set.

To Friedman and his followers, as long as the central bank is able to keep the money supply flowing at a constant rate—say, 3 or 5 percent—then the economy will automatically attain its state of equilibrium without igniting inflation.

This is what monetarists would do when they see a Keynesian shift the AD curve to the right owing to the conduct of *expansionary* fiscal policy: they would just shift it back to its original position. Monetarists believe that if the government has to borrow from the public to finance the budget deficit, it will deprive its citizens of the opportunity of investing their money. Budget deficit would in this case completely crowd out investment.

Or if the effect were not total, it would still be partial.

Other than the crowding-out effect, Friedman also had another trick to downplay the role of fiscal policy. Unlike Keynesians who use after-tax disposable income to explain the behaviors of consumers, Friedman argued that people would rely on permanent income— which is defined by him to be both physical and financial assets as well as human capital in the form of knowledge—to decide what to consume. Since consumption wasn't determined by disposable but "permanent" income, any tax-cut measure by the government would always be considered transitory. In other words, any budget deficit could simply be applied to savings.

Such a belief is also shared by economists who do not consider themselves monetarists. One of them is a Friedman younger colleague at the University of Chicago, Robert E. Lucas Jr., who won the Nobel Prize in Economics in 1995 for his theory on "rational expectations."

In his award-winning work, Lucas uses complex mathematical equations to demonstrate how people, including non-economists, will know *how to predict the future by learning from their past mistakes*. He then focuses his criticism specifically on the conduct of economic policy. If policymakers are uncreative, or repeat the same policy over and over, it is only a matter of time before people will factor the impact into their decisions. So, whenever the government tries to spend more as the means to boost the performance of the economy, people just save—as they're rational enough to foresee that they've higher taxes to pay in the future. Should the central bank increase the money supply, they'll spend and spend by buying lots and lots of things—because they've no taxes to worry about with the "extra" money supplied by the central bank. They'll shift the AD curve—as consumption forms the largest part of it—to the right.

Their archrivals, however, believe in this: whenever the central bank increases liquidity, people would buy bonds instead of going on a shopping spree. This will cause bond prices to rise while interest rates fall. In this case, not only will producers gleefully invest and invest, but also the exporters will be able to export a lot, because when interest rates are low, people in the economy would let their money flow elsewhere to take advantage of high interest rates. That will cause their exchange rates to depreciate, so that their goods become highly competitive on international markets.

Keynesians will therefore shift the AD curve not one but two rounds once there is a change in liquidity. One owes to investment and the other is caused by net exports.

As we can see, economic management must be a wonderful platform for the brightest economists from various schools of thought to showcase their understanding of how an *economy*, as described by Keynes, functions.

They are truly the "masters" in the art of curve shifting.

Of the two variables used to construct the AD-AS framework, we've already eliminated one of them (i.e., the price level). As for the other, economists must have been deliberately or unwittingly omitted something completely when reading *General Theory*. Keynes didn't mention anything about output when formulating his set of equations. It begins with "value of output." As a result, none of them raises a practical issue. *How to value output* as suggested by Keynes before anyone can do anything to his or her economy (if it exists)?

When Lucas got the news from the Royal Swedish Academy of Sciences that he would be a laureate in 1995, he could keep only half of the monetary award, which was 7.2 million Swedish kronor, or about $1 million, because his ex-wife Rita included a paragraph in their property settlement stating that she shall receive half of any Nobel Prize to be won by him in the following seven years.

They divorced in 1988.

Here is a quiz. What was the "value of output" contributed by Rita—who basically contributes nothing at all in the discipline—when Lucas inadvertently allowed someone to profit from half of the reward for his contribution in economics?

No one should ever equate *value of output* to *income*.

The former is a highly subjective concept, whereas the latter is used for the perspective of payee. But no transaction or deal in the human world is unilateral. Workers, landlords, lenders, charitable organizations, and Rita may consider, respectively, wages, rent, interest, donation, and half of the Nobel cash prize or the windfall as their "income," which must be paid or contributed by, respectively, employers, tenants, borrowers, donors, and Lucas.

In monetary terms, income has never been the *sum* of anything (or from the global perspective, it can't even be found in the big, big zero). Should the Department of Defense procure an intercontinental ballistic missile that costs $25 million, the subject of this exchange is an output that could kill tens of millions of people at the blink of an eye on the one hand while the military contractor gets an amount of money on the other (unless the former is unscrupulous and the latter is gullible). Of the $25 million, which is *income* to the recipient, no one is able to tell precisely what part of it is *consumption* so that he or she could determine the amount of *investment* or vice versa. Similarly, it does not depend on how much the government is behaving like a "consumer" or in what part it looks like an "entrepreneur."

Amazingly, most people, including our national leaders, have been led to believe it is the sacrosanct role of the government to manage and control the "one" thing that is essentially no difference from hell or heaven.

No one knows exactly where or what it really is.

The big picture painted by Keynes, in truth, consists of five distinct components that bear no relationship whatsoever with one another in the world where all economists live (or in any dictionary).

8

LIES, LIES, AND MORE LIES

In every economically well-to-do country, it has a department that specializes in data collection. Its primary function is to generate some numbers for people as well as the government to read. The most popular barometers include consumer price index (CPI), producer price index (PPI), unemployment rate, stock indices, and something that everyone should be concerned with. It indeed often gets on the nerves of our national leaders whenever it is not preceded with a positive sign: economic growth.

Basically, its measurement is based on the value of the so-called gross domestic product (GDP), which is the total value of output as defined by John Maynard Keynes in *General Theory*; so that if the GDP of a country was determined to be $105 billion this year and $100 billion last year, then the nominal growth rate of the country for this year is 5 percent.

The computation of a rate is simple. Anyone can do it as long as someone is able to provide him or her with the GDPs of two years. But the value of output is not their ultimate concern because, as noted, economists are only interested in what happens to the "output" level when some of them shift the AD curve or/and the AS curve. They therefore ask statisticians to segregate the GDP into two parts. One goes to price level and the other is called *real output*, which is quite similar to the concept of real money developed by Milton Friedman (which involves price level too).

To get the latter, statisticians would have to determine inflation, which is a rate based on changes in price levels of two years (not the amount of money handed out to the public by the central bank to please its government, as we saw in chapter 6). If the rate of inflation in the country this year is 3 percent, then the growth rate of the real output this year is 2 percent. That is to say, if the inflation in the year is 5 percent, then the country sees "no" growth at all in its real output.

While people may be expected to work really hard to keep the economy afloat (i.e., not to let it drown below zero), statisticians are not compelled to be obediently subservient. With a bit of initiative, they could cut their workload by half. Just gather data on output alone, so that if it is determined to have been 97 billion tons this year and 100 billion tons last year, then the growth rate can be instantly computed. It would "naturally" become *real* (as they do not have to include something that is to be totally excluded later).

So if our economy suffers a negative growth rate of, say, 3 percent, then we have 97 percent of the physical amount of output produced in the previous year to enjoy in this year—as long as the data gathered by statisticians are reliable. Other than this, life moves on.

In fact, the growth rate is just a number that is always related to the past. By the time it's computed, *everything is over*. Yet everyone is so concerned about a value that has never been too far away from zero (i.e., economic growth).

When statisticians map out the output levels over a long period of time, their charts often show that there is "a snake crawling in a tunnel." It is a kind of wave-like shifting between contraction and expansion. Economists describe this kind of boom and slump as *business cycles*.

It's bad for the "economy" if the growth rate is negative—as its output level *falls*.

In *General Theory*, Keynes attributed the Great Depression to aggregate demand being low. In his view, it was largely caused by lack of investment. From then on, economists will simply associate an economy slump with "falling output level."

Given that such a belief has been backed by statistics, let's consider this: if all the outputs produced in a country this year—be it 102, 100, or 97 billion tons—are just sufficient to meet the aggregate demand (that is to say the goods produced were all sold), then by any definition the country should have no recession or depression.

Apparently the cause of an economic downturn is never related to the data gathered by statisticians.

In the human world, people have been turning what's rightfully belonging to nature into all kinds of goods and services for them to conduct exchanges. In the name of *competition*, producers will have to constantly invest to meet the ever-increasing demands of consumers. Other than utilizing the reserves set aside in past years, firms could turn to banks to secure the funds. If bankers share their optimism, they would then grant loans and/or invest in the stocks and bonds issued by these firms.

At the same time, banks could also lend money to those consumers who wish to invest for their future and/or consume now and pay later.

These transactions will cause the size of the big, big zero in the global banking system to *grow*.

In an ideal scenario, money borrowed from banks eventually heads back to their books for *destruction* once human exchanges have been duly completed.

Sad to say, not all human decisions are sound or sensible.

When the urge to invest has become a fad or norm in the business world, it's just a matter of time when it will be flooded with many goods and services that come with various brands and better features. Under stiff and intense competition, firms may have to offer massive amounts of discounts to attract customers. Things will still be fine if the revenues, though reduced, are still able to cover all the overhead costs of doing business. But if they fall below the costs and the hopes of profits are beyond reach, these loss-ridden producers and service providers may have no choice but to wind up their businesses.

Once producers as well as consumers default on their loans, banks will suffer, too. From there on they would raise the threshold on the loans while charging the borrowers exorbitant interest rates. In this case, producers will react by putting their investment plans on hold, while high-end consumers may have to give up their splendid lifestyle that will be "paid for" in the future. Consequently, more assets are written off in the books of banks than created. That will cause the quantity of money held by people to start to fall.

And the worst is far from over.

When the sum of defaulted loans causes the equities of some of them to totally vanish, then banks will become extremely selective in accepting one another's liabilities. That means money, in the form of bank liabilities, *is no longer that generally acceptable*. People therefore might not be to able conduct exchanges freely.

Once a large number of nations are suffering from the kind of scenario just described, then the size of the big, big zero in the global banking system could shrink dramatically over a long time. The combination of these awful incidents would then become the most frightening scenario that the modern civilized world could ever encounter—worse than the Great Depression.

During the great economic turmoil of the 1930s, all the governments of the badly affected Western countries chose to stay away from the dreadful event because they weren't surrounded by Keynesians, and monetarism was an alien term. Today we find our government tasked with generating inflation under the banner of stimulating economic growth. It's therefore unlikely that the Great Depression 2.0 will occur in the near future.

Nevertheless, we can't entirely eliminate short-term economic downturns. If a number of producers and service providers bid good-bye to their workers and staff and you're not among them, it is called a recession. In the event that you lose your job in a retrenchment, it is an economic slump that lasts longer than a recession, and we call it a depression. Stagflation takes place whenever the government feeds the "inflationary" monster, but the jobless people may be too comfortable to be on the dole or just too depressed to look for jobs.

Let's hope people are now familiarized with the true meanings of all these terms used by economists in their scholarly works but that come out of the (big) mouths of politicians to report the economic performance of their country.

Still, whatever the term is, any economic slump will eventually go away. When it's over, no businesspeople and entrepreneurs will ever care about the seemingly inseparable relationship between "productivity" and *competitiveness*. They will just forget how they burned their fingers and do the one thing we shall find *predictable*: once they're back in business for a while, they will begin to expand, invest, expand, invest, and expand some more. Again in no time people will see that these firms have to slash their prices—all because so many goods are produced as well as too many services provided. The recurrences of burned-finger businesses waving good-bye to their poor workers and staff over and over are why the world has the (vicious) business cycles.

Obviously there is no one moment *for the demand of any good— let alone the "aggregate" of all of them—to exactly match its supply* (i.e., to attain the so-called state of equilibrium found in economics). At any given point in time, the world is always filled with all kinds of goods on display and all types of services eyeing for customers.

Or simply put, there is always an amount of "excess" output produced by us.

The question is *By how much?*

Perhaps the department of statistics should survey what portion of the yearly surpluses produced by its country has become unsold goods; unoccupied apartments, offices, and hotel rooms; vacant land, houses, shopping spaces, and warehouses; as well as those restaurants cafés, pubs, and amusement parks and service outlets and facilities that have miserable numbers of customers.

An overall rate of 5 percent simply means that in the year only 95 percent of the output produced in the country is wanted, which we call the *rate of overproduction* (ROOP).

Since we don't live in a perfect world, we shall consider any rate below 2 percent normal. A rate between 2 percent and less than 5 percent is called a recession. If the rate is between 5 percent and less than 10 percent, then it should be classified as a depression.

Once the ROOP has hit double digits, this is another Great Depression.

In this method of measurement, we do not have to consider stagflation—as the rate does not contain prices at all. It is indeed quite different from the one that is currently being practiced by statisticians that uses the previous period as the base in the computation. The output produced in any specified time frame is independent of the rest. That is to say it's perfectly possible for the output produced by a country in a month, a quarter, or a year to be low, and yet it suffers a severe economic downturn.

With a figure that is always positive, ROOP will clearly show us that economic slump is often triggered by nothing but oversupply of output by humans. To eliminate the so-called business cycles, people have to refrain from investment. If the rise of bank assets comes from the *greed* of businesspeople and the *idiocy* of bankers, then the combination of these human traits is the perfect recipe for two kinds of issues commonly found in the human world: *economic downturn,* which is actually caused by excessive amount of unwanted surpluses produced by humankind but always misrepresented in statistics as a negative figure, to be followed by *banking crisis.*

Sad to note, people just listen to a group of scholars who don't distinguish income, value of output, and output in their works and read statistics without questioning them. As such, no businessperson or investor is keen to analyze the true cause of his or her misfortune or losses. Whenever they are presented with a negative figure, they all will just point their fingers at or put the blame on a "term"!

Their national leaders, on the other hand, will vow in front of their electorates that they'll do whatever it takes to battle "falling" output levels.

And this is how they could battle the specter of negative growth. With the backing of the dedicated as well as dependable firefighter-cum-puppet, who is very much enjoying the *unchallengeable power* suggested by Keynes, governments generate inflation. That's why there is a scary "monster" running amok in human societies, which has become the root of a kind of financial turbulence many of us often confuse with "debt": global banking crises.

67

9

THE ROLES OF GOVERNMENT

When John Maynard Keynes wanted the government to save a "term" from drowning in any economic downturn, he must have assumed national leaders are wiser than the rest when it comes to *spending*.

Or conversely, we ordinary citizens, including reputable Nobel Prize laureates, would not be as clever as they are.

In the past, taxes were collected by kings, queens, pharaohs, shahs, emperors, maharajahs, sultans, czars, and other rulers mainly for them to live extravagantly in grandiose castles and palaces as well as to raise powerful armed forces. These human leaders were truly privileged. Not only were others expected to sacrifice their lives to protect their own, they also had the right to decide who was to live or die while enjoying the best of the surpluses produced by farmers, fishermen, winemakers, craftsmen, and many others.

Though they were supposed to take good care of and protect their subjects, some of them turned out to be tyrants, while a few just loved to keep on expanding their frontiers. Those who could slaughter foreign citizens in massive numbers, and then rob their treasures while destroying those they couldn't take away with them, are known in history as conquerors for the empires they built. War was common (as it is even up to today), of which some were fought in the name of religion—which was supposed to cleanse and purify people's minds and souls.

As for modern civilized people living in the so-called free and democratic societies, the elected government should, at least for the sake of courtesy, ask—if it wishes to take something as precious as money away from its fellow citizens.

Regrettably, we do not get this kind of dignity.

Although every constitution will always spell it out rather clearly that *all citizens are equal*, every government in the world is empowered by law to put people behind bars for tax evasion and fine them for late payments. It didn't occur to Keynes when he wrote one of the most "influential" books in history that *taxation was a form of oppression*—a legacy of the past. Instead, he hoped we all would place our faith in its authority without question.

But governments often have trade pacts to negotiate and trade wars to battle. In this case, it must be that our national leaders are unaware of the fact that trade already took place long before any state was formed. If people could exchange surpluses freely in the days of barter, trade barriers must have been erected by those who either show no respect for others' freedom or wish to protect the interests of some privileged while neglecting the others'.

When a handful in a country is given the privilege to spend billions and billions, if not trillions and trillions, of dollars that don't belong to them, we all should have one concern: how to ensure they spend without ulterior motives.

It's hard to imagine that without government there would be no schools, hospitals, roads, or bridges. This is something we all ought to know: no one, in the physical world, would ever become a victim of a robbery where the robber lives in another country hundreds or thousands of miles away. He could be hurt or even killed by someone from around the corner in his neighborhood. Fighting crime should in any case be the top priority of any government.

Sad to say, our national leaders always see something else that no ordinary citizen is allowed to question (owing to so-called national security): *the threat of outside enemies.* That's why a significant portion of the budget administered by any government has been, and will be, spent on a special kind of surpluses, where none of them, including those that may have already been secretly positioned in outer space, has ever been designed to protect us from an alien invasion.

The targets of these kinds of outputs are, alas, members of the human race.

Our world now has a stockpile of weapons of which some are so powerful that, should they ever be detonated, they could blow apart one of the planets in the galaxy known to house intelligent life capable of producing weapons of mass destruction.

This particular kind of output is something that the world will never ever encounter shortages (they are produced all because our national leaders have the "vision" to identify the threat *no matter who their enemies are*). Let us suggest a way for all statistics departments worldwide to measure how our societies use scarce natural resources to produce them. Take the total number of weapons and all the ammunition stockpiled by all governments and then divide it by the world population. A value of 1.2 indicates that the amount of weapons produced by us so far is sufficient to wipe out our own race 1.2 times. A value of 2.4 shows that the "velocity of killing" is 2.4 of all living beings on earth.

Though the rate could well turn out to be "astonishing" (if statisticians are really good at collecting useful and undistorted data), no government is prepared to stop throwing huge amounts of money toward building military strength or superiority and spending on the development, research, and production of more and more high-tech weapons that aim to kill "foreigners" and destroy their property.

Without them knowing (again), all taxpayers, regardless of their nationalities, have become potential enemies of one another. (In some cases, soldiers may be ordered by their "parents" to shoot at their own "siblings.")

No one is exempt.

This is what people will get when their national leaders don't see eye to eye with one another, for any cause: ordinary citizens can be mobilized for a kind of extremely well-organized "gang fight," which we call war. People who do not pledge their allegiance to the same national flag or sing the same national anthem would be expected to blindly kill or be killed by order of their respective national leaders—*even though these people might not have met one another in their entire lives.*

But when these statesmen hug and chat in summit, guess what. They never fail to impress the world how strong the tie they have forged for their countries (through their "constructive talk" with matching ties). By building and deploying forces armed with all kinds of powerful and deadly weapons, it becomes their sole mission to maintain regional—or even global—"peace and stability." Their clichéd and rhetorical joint statement or press release, needless to mention, will become headline news for global citizens to watch and renowned political analysts in international affairs and journalists alike to analyze and debate about. None of them raises a simple fact: only living people can become acquaintances, coworkers, accomplices, lovers, sexual partners, or enemies.

That is to say, *no pair of countries can ever do any of these things.*

Many well-educated modern people, however, are prepared to fight or sacrifice their lives in the name of some "names" printed on a world map, or of religion, or of something else. That's why killing is not a crime but rather a glory or an honor as long as it's carried out with a blessing from or mission issued by some powerful figureheads.

Apparently humans have a kind of hierarchy that is unlike any other. It has two distinct tiers. At the top are the manipulative; at the bottom will be those who are powerless to do anything or who could be rather easily manipulated.

Many of the words that people use—if we were to strip them to the barest elements—*have no substance.* Yet people often use them as though they are "real." When these hollow words are used to form ideas, systems, knowledge, or even inspiration, here is the outcome: no one cares about what's beneath the various acute human issues (while some think they've found the solution or solutions). One particular group of people has indeed been benefiting greatly from this kind of delusion, where truth can be overwhelmed by words. They are professionally trained in reading and interpreting legalese.

This is what makes them noble. When a man is caught red-handed for doing something unlawful, he will not be escorted straight to court to stand trial before a judge, where punishment could be delivered instantly. Rather, someone will have to be present in the court to speak on his behalf.

And the case can last for months or torturous years.

The criminal did commit the crime. If he can't comprehend the charge, then it must be the sole duty of the government to redraft a set of criminal laws in plain, simple language for all accused arsonists, shoplifters, thieves, kidnappers, robbers, looters, molesters, murderers, rapists, serial killers, terrorists, people who cause death to others not for self-defense, and those who damage others' properties to easily understand the charges. If the accused is in doubt of them, he can just grab a copy of a dictionary at a nearby bookstore, surf the internet, or consult a language teacher. If the criminal can't speak at all, then he certainly needs help. The assistance, however, shouldn't be provided by attorneys—unless the *fact* of the case can be altered by the words articulated by them in court.

Any righteous person, irrespective of his or her "profession," should stand up for the accused if he or she is convinced that the charge is groundless.

No one should gain from upholding justice—*if it is truly just.*

Any person who is suspected of committing a crime should be summoned directly by the court to answer the charge in person, because the police possess the evidence against him or her (that means they have no right to detain the suspect to get confession by interrogation). It is then the duty of the judge or the jury (one of them will do) to listen to the accused, who will be allowed the "right" to get help from any source to prove that he or she is the "wrong" person identified by the police, and be convinced that he or she is not telling lies, hiding the truth, or both. Otherwise, the punishment, which should have been stipulated clearly for the charges filed, will be adjudged accordingly.

If the suspect is elusive, then the police will have a warrant to handcuff him or her to the court, where the job of the judge or the jury should become easy—if the suspect can't give a satisfactory explanation as to why he or she chooses to "run away" from justice.

But this is not what we get when the government is tasked to uphold justice. A suspect may be acquitted not because he or she is proven innocent, but the law enforcement officer forgot to mumble some words near his or her ear when he or she was arrested. This shows that judges, *who are supposed to deliver justice*, are not expected to be truth-seekers. They have the absolute authority to "lawfully" seal the truth without even making any attempt to uncover it. Their job is to go by what's spelled out in the books, where *how to use the brain* is rather immaterial in the entire system.

Yet they are the ones who are given the power to decide on the sentence of, say, "a minimum of one year and up to a maximum of five." If the judge is given this kind of freedom, naturally there is an issue about fairness. The punishment may depend on his or her mood or the look of the convicted.

In the name of justice, a court should only handle cases where damages have *physical evidence*. Its primary role is to punish all evil-minded people who cause harm to others or others' property owing to their negligence or irresponsible acts. Those who have "excess" money to invest but don't wish to watch their hard-earned money vanish right before their eyes should take note. Containing greed is always a good deed, as it could prevent any "economy," or the world, from suffering an economic downturn. People just can't keep quiet about the realized returns of their investment but then make a hell of a lot of noise when it turns sour. It is the responsibility of everyone to learn how to face the consequences of his or her bad (or greedy) decisions.

Law books are indeed signed by a few who wish to see their fellow citizens perceiving innocent foreigners to be much more fearful than local criminals (while allowing diplomats who may break the law to enjoy immunity from prosecution), and later subject to conflicting interpretations by various groups of professionals, where the verdict of a case eventually depends on anything but fact and evidence.

As the most bureaucratic, powerful, and oppressive institution, government is always run by those who, knowingly or unknowingly, hunger for or are obsessed with something that will make them look as though they are "greater" than the others (i.e., *power*).

This is exactly how civilized societies, be it today, two millennia ago, or in the future, work. There are a few who are always on "top" of the rest. Because they are flanked by customs or words written in a constitution on the one hand and forces armed with deadly weapons on the other, they have the right to demand others to be loyal, faithful, respectful, and devoted, and at the same time to make important decisions, some of which could have devastating impacts on the rest of society. One of them is a declaration of war, where well-trained soldiers are "licensed" to kill, and when their troops indiscriminately destroy the property of others, they never have to compensate (while they and their families are always very, very well protected by all kinds of security measures, including the lives of some). To them, sacrifices of others' lives and destruction of their property are just parts of their "grand" vision.

Like it or not, no political system is able to fulfill so-called *equality*—no matter how it's evolved or reformed. Democracy is just another term that has been used by some to let us feel like we are "on a par with everyone else and our leader of the moment, which changes every few years."

In a truly "free and democratic" society, no one should have the power of spending money not belonging to him or her, unless permission is granted by the rightful owner. If not the world will have some wise folks who believe they possess the caliber to lead the others. They seek election to public office by chanting splendid slogans and making all kinds of vote-buying promises. Once elected, they will spend the money of others on milk powder, diapers, gas, housing, and even caskets for some of their citizens, who obviously do not need nuclear warheads to protect their families from the threat of local criminals (or terrorists), while paying quite attractively a group of outstanding scientists to develop a kind of "horrifying" output whose production any righteous and conscientious person should oppose. Some officials even have excess money to sponsor all kinds of costly researches and projects to satisfy a few intellectuals whose minds are stuffed with ideas that most if not all ordinary citizens find they can live without.

Here is an illustrative example. There is a saying among a group of distinguished scientists that the universe was created about 13.7 billion years ago by a "bang." Some therefore come up with a theory for them to explore what formed the mass, such as the earth, the sun, and the solar system.

In 1964 the Scottish physicist Peter Higgs, along with a few of his colleagues, suggested this: when the bang took place, it released a kind of elementary particle that slowed down other subatomic particles to form the mass. They named it the "God particle," which existed only during the process of the creation of the universe. To search for it, a few European nations have pooled their resources to construct the Large Hadron Collider (LHC). Built about 575 feet below ground level within a solid tunnel about seventeen miles in circumference near Geneva, Switzerland, the collider allows protons to accelerate in opposite directions, where the head-on collision could —or should—re-create the conditions of the birth of the universe.

While the discovery should be considered a much-celebrated event in the science community, exactly how much does it "cost" just for physicists to search for the particle, which might—or might not— have existed 13.7 billion years ago.

For those people who have no chance of witnessing the grand "moment" captured in the experiment can only imagine how many of the scarce resources belonging to nature have to be extracted just to ensure that the collider is able to withstand that kind of collision, producing temperatures up to a thousand times hotter than the heat of the burning sun, while the ring is being cooled by super-fluid helium at a temperature that could be colder than that of outer space. The amount must be immeasurable (they are the costliest science experiments ever conducted).

As far as time is concerned, 13.7 billion years seems somewhat like an arbitrary "largest" number. Exactly *where the origin of the bang was* if the universe was truly born at about that time should become another big question. Or we should explore what the something—*which was a kind of space indefinable*—looked like before it gave birth to the universe.

It could be totally empty or filled with something else.

Given that no one ever witnessed how everything was created, perhaps we should strive to be down-to-earth. It doesn't really matter whether the universe was created by a small bang instead of a big bang, or there was no bang at all. We just have to always keep one thing in mind: irrespective of what particles it consists of at present, or have indeed disappeared in the past, or will emerge in the future, *nothing in the universal is eternal* (human civilizations are no exception).

With the support from the only organization that has the financial resources needed to carry out all sorts of spectacular or spooky researches in the name of defense, science, or something else, human knowledge uncovered or discovered by highly specialized experts from various fields of study can mean a lot to some *but is entirely irrelevant to others.*

Yet there are governments that have budgeted to be—or try to be—ahead of others in exploring what's considered by many as the next frontier of humankind: outer space.

The hope is to discover life on other planets or in other galaxies, or to explore the feasibility of migrating humans from earth.

On those brownish, barren, and extremely hostile planets where some space objects have landed, humans can't breathe without life-supporting equipment. And don't forget this: when one day the new "home" has become inhospitable (owing to whatever cause), that planet will not have the kind of *scarce* natural resources, as we call them on our planet, for us to embark on another round of migration.

There is only earth for all plants and creatures to share the atmosphere. But our national leaders only care about the interest of their own nation. They believe there is "something" in it for them to manage and are always paranoid that the world can never be at peace because "countries" could become enemies of one another. So they spend, spend, and spend some more on surpluses that otherwise people may not get them, such as thousands of nuclear warheads, tons and tons of chemical and biological weapons, the God particle, some rocks and soil from Mars, mega constructions and projects, items such as the results of some secretive scientific experiments and researches that may have adverse repercussion on human life or the environment, etc., while allowing their fellow citizens to consume "free" amounts of goods and services via, alas, inflation.

Justice, under their care, has become an incredibly lucrative business for some (they could help those with deep pockets to walk away from murder charges or reckless drivers who caused death in fatal road accidents to get away with fines—where life, ironically, is not priceless in the eyes of the judicial system). Led by this group of visionary figures, people in general just can't be honest, conscientious, considerate, righteous, and kindhearted. In spite of the fact that they enjoy something called *education*, which is quite often a huge part of government budget, well-educated modern people still need to be told what to do and what not to do by rules, regulations, and law.

10

A BIG, BIG CIRCUS

The world is currently plagued by many thorny and intractable issues, of which one is causing the globe to get warmer and warmer (i.e., climate change).

In prehistoric times, our ancestors lived humbly in caves or forests. They constantly hunted to alleviate their hunger, and they slept surrounded by four-legged carnivorous creatures and other dangerous as well as venomous animals. Before they had surpluses to exchange, there was no court, no dictatorship, no exploitation, no hooliganism, no illiteracy, no income gap, no marriage counseling, no massacre, no moral education, no racism, no refugees, no religious conflicts, no strikes, no terrorism, no unemployment, and certainly no weapons to fight wars. They didn't even have to be concerned with the one thing that civilized people may have to fight for with their lives: *liberty*.

We've "everything." And for some causes totally unheard of before languages were developed by people, everyone in the civilized world needs to earn a living (or to put it another way, without money or income they just can't live).

Compared to our long-forgotten ancestors, our materialistic life, as we can witness it with our own eyes, is superb. We use one of the most basic elements to sustain life to wash dishes, cars, yachts, etc.; to fill fountains, waterbeds, pools, and gigantic aquarium tanks; to water gardens, golf courses, and parks; to cool down nuclear reactors; to produce TV game shows such as *Wipeout*; and for daily showers. If the supply of water to our homes or offices is interrupted, we barely know how to function. And to quench our thirst, we turn water into all sorts of beverages, of which one becomes the cause of alcoholism. Our food, on the other hand, has hygiene and nutrition to speak of (most of it is now genetically engineered, and some is meant to boost intellectual or sexual power). It has been refined into so-called cuisines.

We have so much of it that many people often have to closely watch their weight or diet (where a few may need liposuction, and food waste is not uncommon).

Soon, commercial space travel will be launched for wealthy people to watch from above how the earth rotates.

Though economists have been placing "scarcity" as the root of all human issues in their studies, modern, well-educated civilized people must be struggling to cope with a kind of problem that none of their uncivilized ancestors ever had to deal with: *abundance*.

According to the father of modern economics, Adam Smith (1723–1790), our "achievement" could be attributed to two key factors. The first is nothing more than common sense: *division of labor*. It states that productivity could increase tremendously when workers were divided into distinct groups to perform a specialized task. The other is the principle of *self-interest*.

In a passage frequently cited from his *An Enquiry into the Nature and Causes of the Wealth of Nations*, published in 1776, Smith proclaimed, "It is not from the benevolence of the butcher, the brewer, or the baker, that we expect our dinner, but from their regard to their own interest."[31] He believed that above all living beings there would always be an *invisible hand* to guide them to move in all directions, yet they would not bang into one another. As long as all people were left alone to pursue their self-interest, not only would they help to increase the wealth of their nation, they could also help to promote something they didn't intend: social harmony.

Smith's work must have painted a "perfect world" for us to envision, except one particular travesty of history belies his ideal.

While Smith was writing the book, many men, women, and even children were captured by some in broad daylight and shipped from one continent to another. Once traded, these slaves would be forced to work throughout their entire lives but never had a chance to taste freedom. Some of them were chained to work, while many others died of exhaustion. It was only in 1807, seventeen years after Smith passed away (and thirty-one years after *The Wealth of Nations* was published), that the British Parliament outlawed the slave trade within the British Empire.

Slavery itself was not abolished worldwide until much later. Even today working conditions in some nations constitute only a modest improvement over bondage. The self-interest of slaves, who were human beings but were a symbol of "wealth" in the eyes of their owners, must have been completely discarded by Smith in his work.

His *Wealth of Nations*, nonetheless, has become the bible of the laissez-faire economic system—or *capitalism.*

The "division of labor" practiced in the civilized world must have bred a few distinctive groups of people. One is allowed to exploit the less privileged and the weaker in the name of "self-interest," while the other group can gain fame by producing scholarly works. (Here is another: the wise and capable.)

Obviously the key to the incredible transformation from almost having nothing to becoming spoiled with choices by humans must be owing to something else altogether.

Ever since people knew how to plant crops, irrigate farmland, and domesticate herds; build roads, bridges, canals, and cities; transport materials, goods, and free laborers (slaves); arm soldiers to battle one another; and so on, nature has been incessantly losing its possessions, including fresh air and clean water, year after year. In the early days, the rate was rather insignificant, but it quickly picked up in momentum as the capability of men to generate surpluses became more and more phenomenal. It took a great leap about 250 years ago, when energy was first used to power machinery (i.e., in the industrial revolution). Since then, the surface of the earth has been changing so rapidly that today there would be little to recognize for those who lived before the machine age.

Perhaps we can compare chain saws and axes to have a better understanding of the point. Production of the latter is simple. It requires only a piece of wood and a piece of metal, whereas factories have to be constructed and machinery as well as equipment have to be manufactured to produce the former. On top of all this, all processes in the production of a power saw and its application require another type of scarce natural resources, where more resources have to be poured in to secure energy. At the end of the day, one of them is far more "efficient" than the other in destroying the kind of scarce natural resources that formed the forests that once covered the planet.

A chain saw is merely one of the uncountable ingenuities of humans. Just to name a few more: If not for Thomas Edison's invention of the light-bulb, half of the planet might not be so easily noticeable from above without moonlight. The dynamite invented by Alfred Nobel must have helped people in many areas. Without it there could be no gigantic dams and tunnels, and many natural resources, such as coal and diamonds, could not be as easily extracted.

An entire aviation industry, commercial or otherwise, was born because the "dream" of flying was materialized by the inspiring Wright brothers in the year when economics became an independent discipline (1903).

As the most powerful driving force beneath the development of civilization, *technology* can never be a "friend" of the environment. It has rather become a tool used by humans to exploit nature. Whenever we have a technological breakthrough (in any area), for sure it is going to suffer badly. Nature will certainly lose many more of its precious possessions (not the five or ten times found in the concept of the income or the money multiplier developed by a group of well-respected and distinguished scholars, but beyond what's quantifiable).

There is no one day, now or in the past, when human societies do, or did, not encroach upon the territory of nature. Every facet of civilization, be it architecture, arts, culture, education, engineering, health care, leisure, medicine, military, religion, science, sports, travel, or whatever, is attained at the expense of its well-being.

After a few millennia of progress, half of the planet is now brightly lit during the night, while the other half is full of human properties of all types, forms, and shapes sitting on land that used to be covered by forests (or belonged to nature), of which there are aquariums and zoos, where some cute animals are trained to entertain our adorable children. Though these wonderful creatures have no words to express themselves, they have dignity, too. The wild and the ocean are where they belong, we should never let them live in artificial environment to satisfy our viewing pleasure—if we wish to learn *how to distinguish the cause of an issue from its solution.*

When virgin land is cleared or forest is burned, this is how wild plants and animals lose their natural habitats. And when we cultivate, produce, excavate, construct, build, as well as explore, more and more scarce natural resources will have to be consumed or depleted, many of which are not self-renewable.

And that's not the end. There is always one final process to complete the entire cycle of destruction, construction, extraction, production, exchange, and consumption (i.e., *disposal*). Other than goods that have gone into our digestive systems, plus those that are valuable in our eyes (such as diamond jewelry, which could buy us love but also require us to consume many more natural resources to keep them safe), all the surpluses we produce today—much of which may contribute to the *rate of overproduction*—will just be dumped at nature's feet one day in the future.

We may name them junk, trash, rubbish, or garbage.

It is ubiquitous.

Various types of used space objects are now floating right above all of us (the sky used to be enshrined by our ancestors as heaven, but is fast becoming yet another junkyard). Torn national flags, largely forgotten by the adventurous climbers who plant them, can now be found on top of the world: Mount Everest.

For waste that can't be incinerated, such as the buildings of demolished commercial, industrial, medical, military, recreational, residential, sports, and all other constructions, decommissioned tanks, carriers, submarines, fighters, and all kinds of deadly weapons, and all solid waste, which were once considered by some as output in the calculation of the so-called economic growth but may become a negative value in statistics—if we don't find them on land or near the vicinity of our homes, they must be sunk and lying somewhere on the beds of lakes, rivers, seas, and oceans (the dumping cost is rather inexpensive and the unpleasant debris is totally out of sight).

Of the used, unwanted, or useless surpluses that we dump, much of it is highly corrosive, durable, flammable, poisonous, toxic, and radioactive. These harmful materials naturally pose a hazard to all living plants and creatures whose only home is the earth.

At this rate of "growth" achieved by humankind (i.e., to *dispose* after destruction, construction, extraction, production, exchange, consumption, exploration, and overproduction that are carried out 24/7), soon the planet will be running out of space for garbage (i.e., full of trash).

Earth now has a high fever. The total area of its forests keeps shrinking and the giant glaciers covering Antarctica and the Arctic Circle continue to melt—resulting in an ever-rising sea level. A significant portion of its environment is largely contaminated, and the natural habitats of many plants, creatures, and forms of marine life are disappearing fast—resulting in many species becoming extinct while more and more of them are endangered.

Living comfortably in a cozy environment that is distantly remote from nature, survival is no longer an issue to most people (it has indeed become a form of entertainment as reality shows for tens if not hundreds of millions of viewers to watch from the comfort of home). We often take things for granted and have all the time to impress one another with our talent. Some are therefore inspired to be the fastest runners in the world or popular idols, while others think that it is glamorous to perform stuns for publication in *The Guinness Book of World Records*. (A few well-fed but despicable and cowardly individuals prefer to be serial killers, rampant shooters, hijackers, suicide bombers, or terrorists.)

While most if not all national leaders too often look no farther than their own national borders (though quite a few of them also vie for what's "up there"), we'll always do our utmost not only for ourselves but also to provide our children the best in the name of their future, and their children in turn will do exactly the same for themselves as well as for their children, and so on.

Most if not all of us, especially those well-educated and wealthy ones, are always prepared to spend on (or invest in) their children in the hope that they can become "somebody" in the future (or right now; it is extremely rare to have parents teaching their kids how not to compete with others and live a simple life just like their forefathers).

It is a universal culture.

While our poor ancestors who received no formal education in their entire life had nothing to dream about, we're never satisfied with what we have. When our life is good we wish it to get better; once that's achieved, we strive for the best; and from the best we're looking forward to incredible; and so on.

Everyone deserves to have a brighter tomorrow, so they say.

At the same time, we still hope that something could be done to protect the environment by reusing, reducing, and recycling as well; while the idea of *sustainable development* has been popularized by many to justify their ambitious projects and ventures.

Everything that we possess, consume, enjoy, or celebrate is a gift from nature. No product, service, energy, or anything else can be truly *green*—unless it is "invisible" (that is to say, it costs nature nothing).

Maybe a dose of reality would help us grasp the real picture.

The amount of resources we consume in a year could possibly have lasted a lifetime for one of our great-great-great-grandparents (or if we were to trace our lineage all the way back to our ancestors living in the Stone Age, it could have lasted them a few generations). By simple extrapolation, this is what humankind will get by the time our great-great-great-grandchildren appear on the planet. With their knowledge, which will certainly be much more powerful than what we've learned so far, the amount of scarce natural resources to be consumed by them in a single year would have lasted the entire lives of their great-great-great-grandparents (us).

Yet we're always so worried about what to bequeath to our future generations, and will be proud if they're inspired to "change" the world.

Except those who live in the jungle but are often considered to be "uncivilized," *all men owe nature an apology.* They have been consuming more than just water and food since the day they were born and will continue to do so until the day they are laid in their graves. Some, apparently, outshine the rest. At the top of the list are human leaders. With the power to spend money not belonging to them, they've become the most notorious and merciless "intruders" of nature. Others include capitalists, entrepreneurs, industrialists, innovators, inventors, technologists, tycoons, celebrities, and wealthy people who live epic lifestyles, and bright scholars (their brilliant works in whatever field will be considered a form of "knowledge" for others to learn in the name of education).

Ever since humankind has known how to accumulate *wealth*—where the big, big zero, or money, is tainted with the blood of nature—and many other things, such as knowledge, earth has been continuously disfigured.

To measure the collective effort of turning precious natural resources belonging to nature into *output* or *garbage*—depending on your perception—put in mindlessly by humankind, we could count on those objects that are now floating in outer space to piece together one simple figure.

It will show us what percentage of the planet *is still in the territory, untouched state, or possession of nature*—day by day.

We may name the figure Unexploited Nature Index (UNI).

Even if the full coordination needed by the owners of these "costly" outputs cannot be carried out, we can still tell that it is moving away from one number *exponentially* toward another. If the trend is left unchecked, then way before it hits zero, global warming may trigger a mega-catastrophic climate change that will transform the once-biodiversity-rich earth into a place as lifeless as Mars.

Unless from now on we and our children and their children are prepared to stop consuming natural resources beyond what's needed to sustain life, all ecosystems will eventually be disintegrated. The rampant natural disasters happening around the globe are ominous signs of what will happen in the not too distant future (or it is indeed already on the horizon).

Can humans change their mindset and *just leave nature all alone* to stop the UNI from falling any farther?

The life of chimpanzees has remained the same since their closest primate cousins walked out of the forests tens of millennia ago. So far there is no sign showing they are actively looking for a new home or planning for a mass migration—though their habitats have been continually destroyed by an extraordinary species. They don't go after fame, fortune, glory, honor, prosperity, reputation, self-esteem, success, or any of the other things their evolutionary cousins do.

No chimp will ever perform a ritual on any of its members hoping the dead can be elevated to another world. Their bodies will just become part of the recycling process in the natural environment.

If not for us, the planet could remain as magnificent as it was for as long as time permits.

That could be tens of millions of years.

The outbreak of the coronavirus or Covid-19 at the turn of 2020 must be a wake-up call for all of us. People, however, in general are devastated by its economic and social impacts as well as financial losses. Some do not mind to forgo their health (or lives) because they don't wish to see their "economy" stall. To combat the pandemic, governments from all over the world are busy rolling out all sorts of stimulus packages, which are nothing but *inflation*. To salvage it from total destruction by an ungrateful as well as egoistic species before it's too late, nature may infuse a highly infectious and incurable virulent virus into humankind as a means to purge its, alas, "tumor."

The unrivaled vortex of chaos stirred by the microorganisms may be the first to cause the modern human world to topple, it is certainly not the last.

That's what lies ahead on the planet we call Earth.

NOTES

1. Erich Roll, *A History of Economic Thought* (New York: Prentice-Hall, 1942), 61.

2. John M. Keynes, *A Treatise on Money*, vol. 1, *The Pure Theory of Money* (London: Macmillan, 1930), 27.

3. Ibid.

4. Milton Friedman, "Quantity Theory of Money," in *The New Palgrave—Money*, ed. J. Eatwell et al. (London: Macmillan, 1989), 3.

5. Ibid.

6. Ibid., 12.

7. Ibid., 3.

8. Ibid..

9. John K. Galbraith, *Economics in Perspective*: *A Critical History* (Boston: Houghton Mifflin, 1987), 25.

10. Ibid., 272.

11. Karl Brunner, "Money Supply," in *The New Palgrave—Money*, ed. J. Eatwell et al. (London: Macmillan, 1989), 263.

12. Jonathan William et al., eds., *Money*: *A History* (London: British Museum Press, 1997), 16, 18, 23.

13. John F. Chown, *A History of Money*: *From AD 800* (London: Routledge, 1984), 18.

14. John K. Galbraith, *Money: Whence It Came, Where It Went* (Boston: Houghton Mifflin, 1995), 17.

15. Aristotle, "The Politics," in *Early Economic Thought*, ed. Arthur E. Monroe (Cambridge, MA: Harvard University Press, 1965), 20.

16. Galbraith, *Money: Whence It Came, Where It Went*, 17.

17. Henry Thornton, *An Enquiry into the Nature and Effects of the Paper Credit in Great Britain*, ed. F. A. V. Hayek (London: Frank Cass, 1962), 10n. Thornton had a vivid description of these accounts in the old days: "The following custom, now prevailing among the bankers within the city of London.... It is the practice of each of these bankers to send a clerk, at an agreed hour in the afternoon, to a room provided for their use. Each clerk there exchanges the drafts on other bankers received at his own house, for

the drafts on his own house received at the houses of other bankers. The balances of the several bankers are transferred in the same room from one to another, in a manner which is unnecessary to explain in detail, and the several balances are finally wound up by each clerk into one balance."

18. Ibid., 90.

19. Ibid., 92.

20. Ibid., 76.

21. Here is the explanation why "Euro" has been used, and the Eurodollar was truly the first type of Eurocurrency: Its emergence is owed to a ceiling set on interest rates in the US banking system in 1933, one of the few major measures to battle the Great Depression. While the economy has long since recovered, the ceiling set on American interest rates remains. When world interest rates rose sharply in the midst of stagflation during the 1970s, the American firms and citizens transferred their US dollars to European banks to transact while earning higher interest rates.

22. Galbraith, *Money: Whence It Came, Where It Went*, 28.

23. Charles Goodhart, "Central Banking," in *The New Palgrave—Money*, ed. J. Eatwell et al. (London: Macmillan, 1989), 185.

24. Irving S. Friedman, *Inflation: A Worldwide Disaster* (London: Hamish Hamilton, 1980), 8.

25. W. David Slawson, *The New Inflation: The Collapse of Free Markets* (Princeton, NJ: Princeton University Press, 1981), 4.

26. John M. Keynes, *The General Theory of Employment, Interest and Money* (London: Macmillan, 1936), 53.

27. Ibid., 54.

28. Ibid., 64.

29. Ibid., 62.

30. John Hicks, "Mr. Keynes and the Classics: A Suggested Simplification," *Econometrica* (1937): 109.

31. Adam Smith, *An Inquiry into the Nature and Causes of the Wealth of Nations* (1776; Oxford: Clarendon Press, 1976), 26–27.

www.ingramcontent.com/pod-product-compliance
Lightning Source LLC
Chambersburg PA
CBHW060442160726
47992CB00003B/1036